Welcome!

From Broome in the far north to the Flinders Ranges in the south, join us as we explore the most breathtaking destinations across Australia. While many of us travel to escape obligations, journeying around Australia comes with responsibilities. In exchange for traveling in a responsible way, you'll get to experience the very best of this huge country, and leave it in great shape for the next generation, too. We've deliberately left out info on major cities to encourage you to head away from the urban centers to explore the wonders of Australia.

Cover image: Slot Canyon at Karijini National Park - Getty Images - Posnov

Contents

10 Unique Experiences in Australia

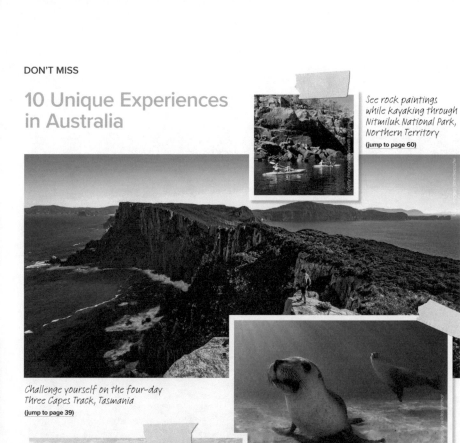

See rock paintings
while kayaking through
Nitmiluk National Park,
Northern Territory
(jump to page 60)

Challenge yourself on the four-day
Three Capes Track, Tasmania
(jump to page 39)

Go diving with sea lions or
sharks, South Australia
(jump to page 54)

Go hiking in Grampians
National Park, Victoria
(jump to page 35)

Take a drive through
the spectacular
Flinders Ranges,
South Australia
(jump to page 55)

003

DON'T MISS

Spot big crocodiles
and tiny tree frogs
in the Daintree
National Park,
Queensland
(jump to page 42)

See natural and artificial
pink lakes, Western
Australia

(jump to page 63)

Explore the incredible
Walls of China,
Outback NSW
(jump to page 30)

See the incredible sandstone
formations of Kings Canyon,
Northern Territory

(jump to page 60)

Stand inside the
red-rock amphitheater
of Cathedral Gorge,
(jump to page 67)

004

Where to Stay

Australia has a wide variety of places to stay to suit all budgets, from high-end luxury and beach houses, to campgrounds and hostels.

With festivals and events on year-round, it's important to find out what's going on, and book accommodation well in advance for big events like New Year's Eve in Sydney.

New South Wales mid-North Coast

Milly McGrath

Hostels

Hostels can vary greatly in standard and size, so look at reviews and ratings on online booking sites, and social media. At a minimum, they will offer free WiFi, a kitchen, shared bathrooms, and several dorm rooms, and should be cheaper than hotels.

Flats and house sharing

If you're looking to stay longer than

Getty Images/Westend61
Streets of Newtown, Sydney

a few weeks, think about house sharing which can be the most affordable option for travelers and easier than trying to find a house with locals who don't want to search for a new flatmate every few months. Try flatmates.com.au or Domain. com.au to search for rooms, as well as Gumtree, the Australian equivalent of Craigslist.

Rent can be quoted weekly or monthly (it varies between cities), and the bond (deposit) is usually four weeks or one month's rent. If you have an informal or short-term agreement, try to negotiate on price. Breaking formal leases can cost you up to six weeks in rent (again, it varies by state), so make sure you know what you are agreeing to.

Hotels and B&Bs

Hotels and bed and breakfasts in

> ❝ Hostels can vary greatly in standard and size, so look at reviews and ratings on online booking sites, and social media.

Australia can be booked through the standard international booking sites; booking.com, hotels.com, Expedia, and TripAdvisor. Prices will climb when big events or festivals are on, so set a price alert if you're working to a budget. Prices should be inclusive of goods and services tax (GST) and not have any other costs on top unless you want parking, breakfast, or other services not included in the price.

Outside of major cities, Australia has many affordable roadside motels and accommodation in pubs. It's worth booking or calling ahead, as towns can be long distances apart, and you don't want to be stuck without somewhere to stay.

Manly beach and the city beyond, Sydney
Getty Images/Spaces

AirBnbs

Airbnb and other accommodation sharing sites are legal in Australia, although different states have different rules governing short-term rentals, and those rules continue to evolve. In major cities, you might be able to find better-priced accommodation in the suburbs, so do a little research to make sure there's suitable public transport to get to the things you want to see.

Camping

With so many national parks and wide-open spaces across Australia, you'll find numerous camping grounds outside of major cities and regional centers. Most campsites will have a website and can be booked in advance. Popular campsites might

book out early when events are on, in particular, music festivals. It's often illegal to camp on beaches or in national parks without a permit, so always check online or with the locals before you set up camp. The National Parks and Wildlife Service website has details of campgrounds in national parks around the country, which are often in beautiful locations.

Budgeting for Your Trip

Generally, the east coast is the most affordable to travel, the west coast is the most expensive, and the Outback falls somewhere in between. Sydney has become the most expensive city in Australia, followed by Melbourne, Darwin, Brisbane, and then Perth. Western Australia is generally more expensive than the other states. Expect costs to increase the further from major towns and cities you travel. In the far north and extreme south, fuel will cost a little more.

To cut costs, research ways to work as you travel, drink glorious goon (cheap wine in a cardboard box), eat two-minute noodles, and ask around hostels to see if backpackers are willing to share their contacts for car-sharing, or give you free camping gear that they don't want to take home.

Never underestimate the hospitality of Australian people, many of whom offer couchsurfing and friendly advice.

Transport

Australia is made up of six states (including the island of Tasmania) and two territories, with 85% of the population living within 31mi (50km) of the coast. To see all 2,969,907mi^2 (7,692,024km^2) that make up Australia's massive continent, you'll need a significant amount of time. Don't set unrealistic goals to see the whole country in three months – it's just not going to happen.

Melbourne CBD
Getty Images/iStock

Going from Perth in the west to Sydney in the east is a long journey, and there's a whole lot of nothing in between. The huge red Outback desert cuts a gigantic swath through its middle, where Uluru is in the middle of nowhere. With so much ground to cover, there are many ways to get around. Some methods of transport are fast and expensive, others are much slower but will save you a lot of your hard-earned money.

During the high season, especially around Christmas and New Year holidays, you'll want to plan ahead. Accommodation books out months in advance, especially in Sydney. While the summer months provide the best weather, it also means peak tourist season; spring and fall may be your best bet to avoid heavy crowds.

> While the summer months provide the best weather, it also means peak tourist season; spring and fall may be your best bet to avoid heavy crowds.

Public transport cards around Australia

Opal Cards can be used on all Sydney trains, buses and ferries, Trainlink services, all buses in the Blue Mountains, Central Coast, Hunter and Illawarra regions, Sydney Light Rail and selected private ferries.

In Victoria, a myki card can be used for trains, trams and buses in Melbourne and regional Victorian centers.

Getty Images/Jodie Griggs
Flying over Brisbane

Camper trailer, Western Australia

Getty Images/Jill Harrison

Use a Go Card on all Translink buses, trains, ferries and tram services around Brisbane, Ipswich, the Sunshine Coast and Gold Coast.

Use a prepaid Greencard to access transport in Hobart, MyWay will give you access to all buses in Canberra, a Metrocard will get you around the city of Adelaide via train, tram or bus, and a SmartRider card will get you onto the public transport in Perth. In Darwin, purchase a Tap and Ride card to make catching buses easier – this can also be used in Alice Springs.

Domestic flights

Moving from city to city and state to state by domestic flight is the most time-efficient way to see Australia. Unfortunately, it's also the most expensive. Qantas and Virgin Australia are the biggest carriers, while Jetstar, Tigerair and Regional Express (Rex) will get you there, too – usually for less money and a bit less reliability.

If you fly, be sure to check the carrier's luggage weight limits, as many restrict carry-on bags to 7kg (15 pounds) in economy class, charging extra fees if your bags weigh more. Weight restrictions drop further when you're catching regional flights.

Bus or coach

Traveling by bus is the cheapest way to get around, particularly if you're backpacking. Sit back, relax and admire the vast open road as someone else does the driving for you. However, be warned, bus journeys are long, so make sure you have something to keep you entertained and travel in comfortable clothes.

Greyhound Australia is the country's largest coach operator, and the only long-distance national coach operator running services in all mainland states and territories. Choose a specific one-way or round-trip ticket or purchase one of

66

Moving from city to city and state to state by domestic flight is the most time-efficient way to see Australia.

Greyhound's Whimit passes. Choose the time period that works, ranging from 7 to 21, 45, 60, 90, 120 or even 365 days, and just go. It gives you unlimited consecutive travel on luxury buses, tricked out with air-conditioning, restrooms, WiFi and USB ports. It has coaches running all over the country, as long as you have the time, they've got the coach to get you there.

Many other tour companies offer comfortable coaches and guided tours in different parts of the country, often with local Indigenous guides who will spark your imagination by weaving Dreamtime stories into the experience.

The Ghan Railway, near Alice Springs

Getty Images/FlledIMAGE

Train travel

Train travel will be slightly more expensive than taking the bus, but dining cars, lounges and sleeping berths on some routes make it a more civilized way to go.

NSW Trainlink has connections throughout the state and into neighbouring Victoria, Queensland and ACT. In Victoria, V/Line operates regional train services throughout the state.

QueenslandRail covers a wide network of tracks that can take you from the Gold Coast to Kuranda, or Rockhampton to Winton.

Trains operate throughout Western Australia, linking travelers to the Northern Territory and South Australia.

Plus, certain trains are filled with romance and hark back to days gone by, rolling along tracks constructed in the 1870s that trace the railroad routes that opened up the country to European settlers. To experience that history, ride The Ghan, the legendary four-day, three-night journey from Darwin to Adelaide (or vice versa), complete with luxurious sleeping cabin, fantastic food, and tour stops along the way.

The Indian Pacific is another luxury train that rumbles coast to coast, between Perth and Sydney, from the Indian Ocean to Pacific Ocean, on a four-day, three-night adventure. The route opened in 1970, connecting the east and west coasts on a single train for the first time.

Driving

Get used to driving on the left-hand side of the road so you can explore Australia by car or campervan (what

"
The Indian Pacific is another luxury train that rumbles coast to coast, between Perth and Sydney

Manly Beach

Useful Apps for a Road Trip Around Australia

There are plenty of mobile phone apps to help guide you along the way, to campgrounds, caravan sites, national parks and must-see sights, too. Try WikiCamps Australia for places to camp; HemaExplorer to download offline maps so you're never lost, even if your phone signal is gone; and Star Walk 2, the fantastic stargazing app that shows you every constellation in Australia's Southern sky.

Aussies call motorhome RVs), the best way to explore everywhere from big cities to places so remote you'll wonder if there's anybody out there.

For easy exploring, simply rent a car at the airport and go, finding accommodation along the way or booking it in advance. Always choose a full-to-full fuel policy, be flexible with your pick-up location, keep the number of drivers to a minimum, and beware of extra surcharges. Read your car hire paperwork thoroughly to be sure you aren't caught out on any sneaky details.

If you're planning on an extended trip, you may find it cheaper to buy a car or campervan. Check hostel/ campground notice boards for vehicles for sale, and once you're done with it, sell it the same way you bought it. You'll need to have car insurance to drive legally, and in case of any emergencies.

Check out online carshare options such as Car Next Door or Drive My Car to see if you can save money and get around cheaper. These peer-to-peer services are best for those who are getting around major cities, but won't be of much help for those of you who are doing longer road trips.

Mobile reception in Australia can be spotty, especially in the country and Outback. Carry a paper map, let someone know where you're heading, and when to expect your return, and always fill up the petrol tank whenever you pass a petrol station in remote areas – sometimes it could be hundreds of miles before the next one. Always keep an eye out for wildlife on or beside the road, especially kangaroos which are most active at dawn and dusk, and can cause a major accident if hit.

Festivals Calendar

Australians love a party, so it should come as no surprise that the festival scene is as eclectic as the landscape that's the backdrop for many of the country's best events.

Music festivals

New Years Eve's annual Falls Festival has expanded from the Victorian town of Lorne to beachside towns in three other states: Marion Bay (TAS), Byron Bay (NSW), and Fremantle (WA). The three-day festivals have a Glastonbury vibe, with camping, great headliners, and a convivial atmosphere.

Tamworth Country Music Festival has been celebrating the sound and spirit of the bush each January since 1972. In addition to big international and local names, the NSW town gives itself over entirely to the festival, with multiple buskers and extra events.

WOMADelaide is a contemporary music festival of global sounds and conscious living for all ages, held in Adelaide's Botanic Gardens each March.

In April and May, Groovin the Moo music festival is held over three weekends in the picturesque regional centers of the Hunter Valley (NSW), Townsville (QLD), and Bendigo (VIC).

Also in April, Byron Bay Bluesfest is a relaxed, family-friendly festival and arts celebration. The hippie haven is also home to Splendour in the Grass, with a Coachella-like line-up of musical talent, held each July.

Vivid Sydney

Buskers at Tamworth Country Music Festival

Deni Ute Muster, NSW

Deni = the town of Deniliquin; ute = utility (like an SUV); muster = 20,000 people descending on a small community to celebrate Outback culture.

Two decades ago, when the region struggled through a crippling drought, locals came up with the idea of a festival to generate an alternative source of income to farming, and the uniquely Australian Ute Muster was born. A full program includes chainsaw carving, wood chopping, Australian wildlife shows, and, of course, car exhibitions and racing. The free camping is a bonus after the

Deni Ute Muster

eight-hour drive from Sydney, but don't expect to sleep.

Outback Camel Races, NT

Camels have been raced in the Outback since the 19th century, when, what is now the largest herd of camels in the world, was transported from Asia to be used for labor. Check out the Uluru Camel Cup each May, while the Queensland season begins in July, with weekly carnivals in Bedourie, Boulia, and Winton. As well as the races, there's plenty of food, drink, music and more. Camping is free on site for ticket holders.

Camel in the Outback

Getty Images/mastersky/Beard

Beer Can Regatta, NT

Darwin's Beer Can Regatta started in 1974 when 22,000 people turned out at Mindil Beach to watch boats, made of beer cans, race and often fall apart. Today, it's even more popular and has expanded to include a thong-throwing competition (flip-flops), live music, and plenty of drinking — it's hot up there.

Henley-on-Todd Regatta, NT

The annual Henley-on-Todd Regatta has been held in the Todd River's dry creek bed since 1964. What was once considered a joke to outsiders, who didn't understand that the Todd is usually a waterless riverway, has turned into the only dry boat race in the world. Competitors race their vehicles on foot, like the cars in *The Flintstones*.

Henley-on-Todd Regatta

GettyImages/Lisa Maree Williams

Dark Mofo, TAS

In Tasmania, the winter solstice is celebrated at Hobart's Museum of Old and New Art (MONA) with the 10-day Dark Mofo festival. Ticketed art events and free talks are held around the city, and festival highlights include the Winter Feast, a three-night nod to pagan tradition, and the Nude Solstice Swim in the Derwent River. Brrr.

Elvis Festival, NSW

Every January, the NSW country town of Parkes gets all shook up by the music of The King at the five-day Parkes Elvis Festival. The festival celebrates the music and legend of Elvis Presley with car shows, rock 'n' roll dancing, and

Dark MOFO

Ali Atkinson

couples renewing their vows as Elvis and Priscilla.

Broken Heel Festival, NSW

Disco divas head to this desert festival, in the NSW Outback town of Broken Hill, to celebrate the cult film *Priscilla, Queen of the Desert* which was partly filmed here. For one weekend each September, the festival offers comedy, cabaret and live music. Get in early for tickets on the Stiletto train from Sydney, or look for buses from Adelaide and other major cities.

Wide Open Space, NT

Head to Ross River Resort in the East MacDonnell Ranges, 52mi (85km) east of Alice Springs, each May to experience Wide Open Space, one of Australia's most unique events. Since 2009, this three-day festival has celebrated the unique desert culture of central Australia through music, art and culture, and features a selection of artists and performers who wouldn't normally travel to the Australian Outback.

Sculpture Symposium in Broken Hill

Getty Images/Christopher Chan

Year-round Festivals at a Glance

	ACT	NSW	NT	QLD	SA	TAS	VIC	WA
JAN		Tamworth & Elvis festivals						
FEB								
MAR	Illuminations, Canberra				WOMADelaide			
APR		Byron Bay Bluesfest &		Groovin the Moo, Townsville			Groovin the Moo, Bendigo	
MAY		Groovin the Moo, Hunter Valley	Uluru Camel Cup & Wide Open Space					
JUN								
JUL		Splendour in the Grass, Byron Bay	Darwin Beer Can Regatta	Camel racing season begins				
AUG			Henley on Todd Regatta					
SEP		Deni Ute Muster & Broken Heel						
OCT								
NOV						Dark Mofo, Hobart		
DEC	Design Canberra Festival	Falls NYE Festival, Byron Bay				Falls NYE Festival, Marion Bay	Falls NYE Festival, Lorne	Falls NYE Festival, Fremantle

Indigenous Culture

The essence of Australia's Indigenous cultural treasures lies in the complex relationship between Indigenous people, their connection to Country (the Aboriginal wording for land and living things), and kindred species embraced in totems and spiritual beliefs.

Aboriginal rock art at Carnarvon Gorge, Queensland

Getty Images/SherokeeS

Totems can be a natural object, plant or animal and are inherited by members of a clan group as their spiritual emblem. Totems define roles and responsibilities within the clan, and their relationships with each other and creation. Often called "the Dreaming", these complex spiritual belief systems are the laws Indigenous people live by and the basis for their ability to thrive in a diverse and often harsh environment.

History

Aboriginal Australia has suffered greatly from the impacts of colonization, and understanding some of this history is important for any traveler who wants to understand real Aboriginal Australia. Visitors should learn about the massacres, the policy of assimilation, the internment on missions, the removal of Indigenous children from their families, and the work conditions that occurred on pastoral leases and in domestic service.

Acknowledging Aboriginal people as the Traditional Custodians of Australia demonstrates a positive understanding, and opens doors to an even more valuable Aboriginal cultural experience. In regional Australia, especially where cultural practices are strong, visitors should ask for permission to visit certain places and take photographs.

In 2017, the Traditional Owners of Uluru (also known as Ayers Rock) decided to stop all climbing on the huge sandstone formation, with a ban coming into effect in October 2019. Visitors are welcome to appreciate Uluru as a cultural site, and come ready to listen and learn about ancient wisdom, and connections that go deep into this ancient land. Removal of rocks and artefacts from this sacred region is taboo and considered a great insult to

In 2017, the Traditional Owners of Uluru (also known as Ayers Rock) decided to stop all climbing on the huge sandstone formation, with a ban coming into effect in October 2019.

Traditional Custodians and a breach of cultural lore.

Authentic Indigenous tours

Kuku Yalanji Cultural Habitat Tours in Far North Queensland, offer authentic insights into traditional fishing grounds on a walk through the mangroves. You can also learn how to identify plants used for bush tucker (food) and medicine, and the daily local traditions of the local people.

In Broome, Western Australia, Bart Pigram runs Narlijia Cultural Tours, and helps travelers learn about fascinating stories of life around Roebuck Bay from his unique perspective.

In South Australia, Quenten Agius of Aboriginal Cultural Tours will walk you across the beautiful country of the Yorke Peninsula and Outback South Australia, sharing Dreaming stories that bring the landscape to life, and demonstrate his people's occupation of Country for thousands of years.

Lirrwi Tourism in northeast Arnhem Land, Northern Territory offers adventures in culture, including a day tour to the Bawaka Homeland with a Traditional Owner, or a yidaki (didjeridu) masterclass as part of a small group tour.

In Victoria, look for Brambuk Aboriginal Cultural Centre located in the Grampians National Park (Gariwerd). You can book an Aboriginal rock art tour and try native foods at the café, all while learning about Aboriginal culture.

In Tasmania, book a tour with Wukalina Walk, by Palawa Enterprises, to walk with a Palawa Aboriginal guide while exploring the spectacular Bay of Fires.

Indigenous culture in cities

Take a guided walk through Sydney's Botanic Gardens with Aboriginal Bush Food Experience, and at Sydney's Barangaroo, Aboriginal Cultural Tours show how Indigenous history, culture and connections survive despite urban development.

On Queensland's Gold Coast, experience the interactive Dreamworld Corroboree. In Cairns, millions of visitors have seen performances and dance at Tjapukai Cultural Park.

> You can learn how to identify plants used for bush tucker (food) and medicine, and the daily local traditions of the local people.

Taste Indigenous Food

Native foods are gaining attention for their high nutritional value and unique flavors, with celebrity chefs capitalizing on their exotic and nutritional profiles. Indigenous chefs such as Mark Olive, Clayton Donovan, Rayleen Brown and Josh Whiteland ensure Aboriginal expertise stays front and center of the native foods phenomenon. Kungkas Can Cook in Alice Springs, Koomal Dreaming in the Margaret River region of Western Australia, and Charcoal Lane Restaurant in Melbourne are all worth a visit.

Noma's Rene Redzepi food foraging in South Australia

Unique fruits, vegetables and spices, that have been harvested and traded for thousands of years, are now becoming available to wider markets. While these are seasonal and generally in limited supply, items such as lemon myrtle, saltbush, quandongs and bush limes are in high demand.

Known as emu apples or native cranberries, muntries are a low-growing shrub found on the south coast of Australia. When ripe, the berries are green with a red tinge and have the flavor of spicy apples. These tasty little berries are high in antioxidants, (four times that of blueberries), and can be eaten fresh or used in many sweet and savory dishes.

Sustainable Travel Tips

Beyond the obvious universal commandments of travel (not littering, avoiding plastic bag use, respecting local culture) here are some tips for a low-impact journey Down Under.

Respect quarantine laws

Think that apple in your backpack is no big deal? Think again. As an island nation, Australia has some of the strictest quarantine laws in the world, designed to protect the country's biodiversity, and fines and confiscation of materials are strictly enforced.

Carefully read your arrivals card and declare anything you're unsure about (such as plant materials and food). Beyond airports and state borders, many national parks require hikers to wash their boots to avoid cross-contamination between ecosystems. Many states have

Kangaroo on the beach, Esperance, WA
Getty Images/seanscott

installed vehicle wash-down bays and boot cleaning stations to stop invasive species from entering national parks.

Respecting culture and traditions

From the seafaring saltwater people of the north to the inland communities of the Central Desert, hundreds of Indigenous tribes and language groups make up modern-day Australia.

As always, travel with an open mind, a curious nature, and generous spirit, and you'll be in a good place to learn about Australia's rich Indigenous culture.

Whenever you encounter Indigenous communities, always seek permission before taking photos of people, rock art, and sacred sites. Support Indigenous talent by

> " Beyond airports and state borders, many national parks require hikers to wash their boots to avoid cross-contamination between ecosystems.

Katie McIntosh
Mataranka Thermal Pools, Queensland

016

Bald Head Walking trail, Albany, Western Australia

buying art directly from artists or from galleries that pay artists a fair price for their work. Find Indigenous-owned tour operators to learn from Indigenous guides.

Sidestep that cheap, mass-produced souvenir boomerang, probably made in a factory overseas, and buy the real deal from an Indigenous artisan instead.

Respecting native wildlife and the environment

Leaving a place in the same (if not better) state than you found it is recommended no matter where you are traveling.

Australia's native animals are a big drawcard for visitors, and they deserve to be treated like the animal royalty they are. Even though koalas and wombats look cuddly, they are easily stressed by human interaction, should only be admired in the wild

and not picked up. Avoid wildlife venues that encourage interaction.

When driving in rural areas, be wary of native wildlife which often wanders onto roads. Kangaroos are most active at dawn and dusk, so stay extra vigilant if you are on the road at those times.

Foraging for food might be all the rage in culinary circles, but picking Australian native plants without a license is illegal in most states. Even something as innocent as picking wildflowers can interrupt nature's regeneration cycle.

Fishing without a permit is illegal in many states, so, before throwing in a line, check the local laws and always follow size and bag limits for your catch.

Never remove seashells or coral as a souvenir; make a bigger impact and pick up some litter instead. Australia will thank you for it.

> "
> Foraging for food might be all the rage in culinary circles, but picking Australian native plants without a license is illegal in most states.

Australian Wildlife (That Won't Kill You)

While Australia is well-known for its many dangerous creatures, it is also home to some of the world's most adorable, beautiful, and captivating animals.

Wildlife of the Australian Outback

Thorny devil lizards move across the sand in search for ants, greater bilbies construct extensive underground tunnel systems, and large perentie goannas prey on just about anything they can catch. Perenties have been known to even take down large wombats, kangaroos, and dingoes.

If you camp out in the Outback, you'll hear the howls of dingoes echoing across the landscape. You'll also come across the world's largest herd of feral camels, which were introduced to Australia in the 19th century from India and Afghanistan for transport and work in the Outback. They were replaced by motorised vehicles in the early 20th century and released into the wild.

Wildlife of Tropical North Queensland

Australia's dry Outback interior gives way to the world's oldest rainforest in Tropical North Queensland. A visit to the Daintree Rainforest is like stepping back into the age of dinosaurs.

You half expect to come across a towering T-Rex but instead, you must settle for the prehistoric-looking cassowary. These flightless birds can be more than 6ft (1.8m) tall, and the southern cassowaries of Australia can inflict serious injuries with their dagger-like claws if provoked or while protecting their young. Unlike most birds, it is the male cassowaries that incubate and care for the young, while the females live solitary lives. While their kick may be dangerous, cassowaries would much rather browse the forest floor for various fruits. Give them a bit of space while you admire these giants, with their colorful heads, adorned with extraordinary casques.

Kangaroos take to the trees in tropical North Queensland where, if you're lucky, you might catch a glimpse of a threatened Lumholtz's or Bennett's

Red kangaroos

Megan Jerrard

Eclectus parrot

Megan Jerrard

Koala

Pixabay/MartinStr

tree-kangaroo. You almost wonder if they are trying to climb to get a better glimpse of the shimmering blue Ulysses butterfly or the vibrantly colored Eclectus parrot that grace the canopy.

Wildlife in the Northern Territory
The wetlands of Kakadu National Park are home to hundreds of bird species including brolgas, black-necked storks, and vibrant Gouldian finches. You may also come across a frill-necked lizard trying to steal some of the attention when it displays its threatening mane. As darkness falls, giant flying foxes take to the skies to provide a moving concert of sound.

You might feel quite small in the Top End, due to the sheer expanse of the landscape and also when standing next to the towering natural skyscrapers created by cathedral termites. These termite mounds can reach 26ft (8m) in height and can remain active for up to 100 years.

Wildlife of Tasmania
Australia's island state provides the opportunity to see many species which have become endangered or extinct on the mainland. It's known as the 'land of the devil' after its most notable inhabitant, the Tasmanian devil, a marsupial carnivore with an intimidating personality. This once common, and loveable, species has seen a rapid decline in its population due to a detrimental facial tumor disease that has spread across Tasmania.

While searching for the devil, you will probably come across the adorable small kangaroo-like pademelon, as well as marsupials the potoroo, bandicoot, and bettong.

The island is also home to both of the world's only egg-laying mammals – the duck-billed platypus and the spiky echidna. The platypus, a creature which looks like it was pieced together from a box of leftover animal parts, is generally shy, and often nocturnal on the mainland, but can be spotted more often in Tasmania.

It's too late to spot one of Tasmania's most iconic animals, the thylacine (or Tasmanian tiger). The last known surviving thylacine died in the Hobart Zoo on September 7, 1936. It was declared extinct in 1982.

Cassowary

Frill necked lizard

Tasmanian Devil

Safety

Long stretches of roads through the Outback, dense bush and the freedom to drive, hike and camp (seemingly) wherever you want to might seem like a great idea, but it has caused problems for many unprepared travelers in the past.

Road trip preparation

One of the best ways to experience Australia is on a road trip, but don't underestimate Australia's size, the distances between destinations, and the rough terrain. The best way to ensure road trip success is to be prepared.

It's easy to drive around Victoria, but while the state is compact, the distances can be deceptive, particularly in the High Country where you'll need to drive slowly along windy roads.

There are huge areas of Australia that have no internet and phone coverage, so your smartphone will often be rendered useless. Go old school and carry paper maps as a backup. Always tell someone about your travel plans, so they can alert the authorities if you don't turn up when you're meant to. If you're going off-road, into the desert or camping in remote bushland, consider hiring a satellite phone to stay in touch. Renting a 4WD vehicle is the safest way to experience any road trip that goes into the desert, but ensure you have the latest maps, emergency

Lucky Bay in Cape le Grand National Park, Western Australia

equipment, off-road recovery gear, and stay up to date with information about weather and hazards on the road.

Huge distances between towns means accessing fuel and fresh water can be difficult in the Outback. Avoid being stranded by the side of the road by carrying ample water and fuel to get you through your trip. Crossing the Nullarbor Plain in a banged up, old hatchback you bought off a guy in a pub isn't wise, and could find you becoming the subject of a cautionary tale on the evening news. Instead, hire an all-terrain vehicle well-suited to travel on unsealed roads.

While driving around Western Australia, be prepared for vast distances between fuel stops, communities, and towns with accommodation. Perth to Broome is almost 1,500mi (2,414km), while Perth to Esperance clocks in at 470mi

“ While driving around Western Australia, be prepared for vast distances between fuel stops.

Katie McIntosh
Jumping Crocodile Cruise, Northern Territory

Australian sun. Red, roasted Brits and Europeans on Australian beaches are a common sight, but this can be prevented. Always slip, slop, slap; slip on a shirt, slop on water-resistant, broad spectrum sunscreen (at least 30+) and slap on a hat. It's essential to cover up and protect your skin from the UV rays during the hottest parts of the day (between 10am - 3pm). Seek shade where possible and always stay hydrated.

Sunburn is painful, and can take days or weeks to go away depending on the severity. Melanoma (skin cancer) is a major issue in Australia with an estimated 14,000 cases diagnosed each year.

(756km). Make a strategic plan and plot out the location of roadhouses if you're venturing into remote locations. Most roadhouses offer fuel 24/7, as well as accommodation and bathroom facilities.

Total fire bans

During bushfire season, Australia's dry heat turns the country into a tinderbox. Knowing when a Total Fire Ban is declared is essential. Displayed on local government websites, news bulletins, and highway signage, a Total Fire Ban means exactly that – don't light a fire. Even throwing a cigarette butt out of a car window can have catastrophic results including endangering lives, wildlife, and homes. If you build a campfire (only where and when allowed), always extinguish it properly with water, and bury the embers with soil or sand.

Sun safety

While an Australian summer will do wonders for your tan, don't underestimate the harshness of the

Where not to swim

On a blistering hot day, the rivers, beaches and billabongs of Australia are unbelievably tempting – but think before jumping in. From crocodiles to strong currents and submerged rocks, hidden dangers lurk in Australia's waterways. Always swim between the yellow and red flags at patrolled beaches as these are the designated safe spots, and never swim when you've been on the booze. Read the signs – many rivers and lakes look serene but hide strong currents. Don't put a foot into any body of water in Far North Queensland or the Northern Territory without first asking a local, a ranger or reading signs – Australia's 200,000-plus population of saltwater crocodiles live here but can be avoided by swimming where it's safe.

" On a blistering hot day, the rivers, beaches and billabongs of Australia are unbelievably tempting – but think before jumping in.

Sharks

Despite all the media hype, sharks aren't a big problem in Australia. You're statistically more likely to end up in a car accident going to the beach than being bitten by a shark, however there are things you can do to be shark smart while enjoying the ocean:

- Avoiding the ocean around dawn and dusk is a myth – incidents can happen any time of day
- Don't swim after rain, when run-off reduces water visibility, or if the water is murky
- Avoid areas where there is fish feeding going on e.g. visible bait balls, which attracts smaller marine animals, with larger ones like sharks following too. Birds dive bombing are a clue
- Always swim or surf in a group
- Only swim at a patrolled beach, and obey all directives from authorities if a shark has been sighted, and calmly leave the water
- If a beach is closed, it's closed. Don't disobey the signage or warnings by authorities.

Great White Shark

Getty Images/wildestanimal

Bluebottles and other stingers

Bluebottles are a common sight on Australia's beaches during the summer, with armadas of these iridescent blue, long-tentacled creatures washing up on the beach. Copping a sting is painful, and many people accidentally step on them while walking near the shore, or get stung while swimming in the ocean. If you happen to experience the pain of a bluebottle sting, seek first aid immediately. Don't rub the sting area. Try to pick off the tentacles with tweezers and immerse the sting area in hot water (as hot as you can stand) or pack with ice.

Irukandjis and box jellyfish are mainly found up in the waters of northern Australia and as far south as the Whitsundays, with numbers peaking during November to May, however they are found all year around. Irukandjis are more transparent and smaller than bluebottles, which makes them hard to see in the water, and their sting causes localised pain, disorientation, respiratory distress, and more. Box jellyfish are bigger than Irukandjis, and their sting is reportedly more painful, and causes noticeable wounds.

If you are stung by Irukandji or a box jellyfish, immediate first aid is vital. Call 000 and rinse the area with vinegar. Carefully remove the tentacles with tweezers. Reassure the patient and keep them calm. Perform CPR if necessary until medical help arrives.

You're statistically more likely to end up in a car accident going to the beach than being bitten by a shark.

Visas

If you are not from Australia or New Zealand, you will require a visa and valid passport to enter the country.

Tourism and business visas

For tourism or business purposes, you can apply for three different types of visas: Electronic Travel Authority (subclass 601), eVisitor (subclass 651), Visitor visa (subclass 600).

Before arriving in Australia, all travelers must fill out an Incoming Passenger Card, which includes declarations about health and character. It's important to obey all Australian laws attached to the visa while traveling.

If you overstay your visa, you will face penalties. If you wish to stay longer than your original visa will allow, you need to apply for a further visa. If, however, you have a 'No further stay' condition on your visa, you must leave Australia no later than the date on which your visa ends, and re-apply once you've left the country.

Working holiday visas

Living and working in Australia is a dream for many travelers, and you can make it reality with a working holiday visa. If you're under the age of 31 you may qualify to live and work in Australia for up to two years.

Australia has two different Working Holiday Visas: Subclass 462 and

Hikers on Fraser Island

Getty Images/bomsie009

Subclass 417. Check online to see which visa subclass your nationality qualifies you for. Many nationalities can apply online through the Australian Department of Immigration and Border Protection website. However, not all can apply online and must instead file a paper application. Check the Department of Immigration website to see if you can apply for your visa online.

Some nationalities must lodge their visa applications at the Australian Immigration office within their own country or a nearby country. Not every applicant will be accepted for a Working Holiday Visa. Some countries have a limited number of visas available per year. But you won't know if you don't try!

> Living and working in Australia is a dream come true for many, and you can make it reality with a working holiday visa.

Weather

Don't ruin your chances of reaching incredible national parks in Australia's far north during the wet season or missing out on hiking in Tasmania during winter; plan ahead for all your activities by choosing the best season for your destinations.

Dawn in the bushland of the Northern Territory

The Top End

The Northern Territory, Far North Queensland, and northern reaches of Western Australia all experience the wet season from November to April, with high humidity, scorching temperatures, and heavy rainfall. Travelers should expect some roads to be closed because of flooding, and be aware that tropical cyclones could form off the coast of Australia, causing widespread damage across the region. The wet season is a great time for photography with lightning flashing across darkened skies and raging waterfalls.

The dry season, from May to October, sees low rainfall, and low humidity. Waterholes and rivers in this area dry up, making access to the remote spots of the Northern Territory much easier.

Western Australia

Perth enjoys hot, dry summers and mild winters. Be prepared for heavy rain and potential thunderstorms during winter (June to August), when the temperatures inevitably drop.

From December to February, Perth doesn't receive much rainfall, so your chance of catching an incredible Western Australian sunset over the ocean are high.

Queensland

The climate on Queensland's southern coast ranges from comfortable cool temperatures in winter to hot and dry summers. Warm temperatures both in and out of the sea can be enjoyed throughout the year, keeping keen surfers, hikers and swimmers happy, year-round.

New South Wales

The seasons in New South Wales are usually pretty predictable, with occasionally freezing temperatures in winter, scorching hot summers, moderate weather in fall, and

> The dry season, from May to October, sees low rainfall, and low humidity. Waterholes and rivers in this area dry up, making access to the remote spots of the Northern Territory much easier.

(arguably) the most enjoyable climate in spring. Of course, don't expect to have the beaches and hiking trails to yourself during the months of December and January, when tourists flock to Australia for the warm weather. But, if you find some hidden gems along the NSW coast, you'll be able to enjoy warm temperatures and no crowds.

Victoria

During winter (June, July and August), it's the perfect time to head to the ski fields of the Victorian High Country. Melbourne's weather is famously temperamental, with wild winds, heavy rain, and freezing temperatures surprising locals year-round. Don't be surprised if insane heat waves bring the city to a halt in summer – remember, you're in Australia. When the weather is warmer in December, January and February, head to the coast for a surf or enjoy a beautiful coastal walk along the Mornington Peninsula.

South Australia

South Australia experiences mild winters and a warm, dry summer. Rainfall is sparse from December to February, and temperatures will occasionally soar above 104°F (40°C). Try visiting in fall (March to May) for pleasant weather and very little rainfall. Snow is rare in South Australia, but occasionally the Adelaide Hills will receive a dusting between the months of June and August.

Paragliding at Stanwell Tops, New South Wales
Getty Images/Adnan Vejzovic

Tasmania

The weather in Tasmania can often change dramatically without much notice. Just in case, always pack wet weather gear and warm clothes. Tasmania will also, quite literally, blow you away with strong gusty winds – known as the Roaring Forties – and the west coast is famous for its torrential rain.

Summer runs from December to February, and is typically the best time to go hiking. From March to May, the leaves turn red and yellow. If you want to see humpback whales on their migratory path, visit during May, June and July, or later in the year between September and November.

Temperatures drop in winter (June to August), and snowfall turns the wild landscapes into a snow-covered wonderland.

> " Of course, don't expect to have the beaches and hiking trails to yourself during the months of December and January.

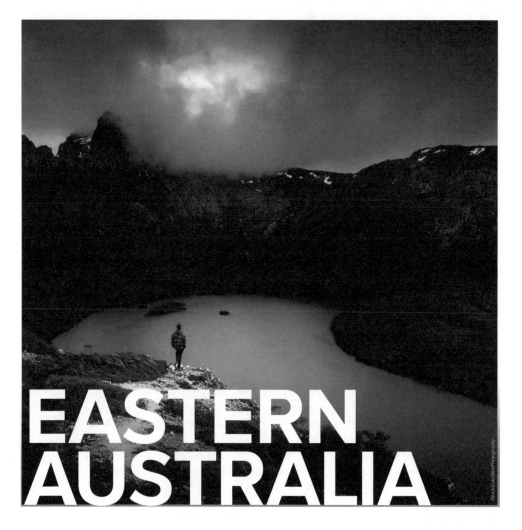

iStock/LukeWestPhotography

EASTERN AUSTRALIA

From the country's longest and deepest cave systems in Tasmania, the tropical landscape of the Daintree Rainforest in Queensland and the laid-back country and beach towns of New South Wales, Australia's east has so much to explore on land and water; you just need to know where to go. You'll probably arrive in Sydney, Melbourne or Brisbane, but then head out of the city to have an Australian-sized adventure.

New South Wales

Home to some of Australia's best beaches, hundreds of national parks, six World Heritage Areas, and fascinating Outback towns, New South Wales is best explored by car. Rent a car in Sydney and set off to explore the state with your own set of wheels.

Blue Mountains National Park

Explore the Illawarra region

Drive south of Sydney to explore Royal National Park with its miles of bushwalking tracks and beautiful beaches. The world's second-oldest national park is great for hiking, mountain biking, surfing, and whale watching. A little further south the dramatic Grand Pacific Drive takes in the quiet surf towns of Thirroul, Austinmer, Stanwell Park and Coledale. You can go skydiving over Wollongong, visit Dharawal National Park for hiking and wild swimming, hang gliding in Stanwell Tops, and head to Budderoo National Park for a birdwatching rainforest walk.

Blue Mountains National Park

Each year, millions of people head west from Sydney to the Blue Mountains to see the famous Three Sisters in the World Heritage-listed Greater Blue Mountains Area. Escape the crowds in Blackheath to enjoy great food and the breathtaking views of the Grose Valley from Evans Lookout. Or, if you're up for a challenge, hike down the Golden Stairs and climb Mount Solitary for 360-degree views down the Megalong Valley.

On the western edge of the Blue Mountains, you'll find the country town of Lithgow. Nearby, Hassan's Walls Lookout is the highest in the Blue Mountains, offering panoramic views of the national park. An hour south, Jenolan Caves is a 24mi (40km) network of ancient limestone caves containing Silurian marine fossils and massive calcite formation. But, if you want a cave experience without the crowds, head 40 minutes north of Lithgow to the Glow Worm Tunnels in Newnes Plateau.

Kangaroo Valley and Jervis Bay

In the Shoalhaven region of NSW, about two hours from Sydney and Canberra, Kangaroo Valley is a lush paradise of rainforests and green pastures, perfect for camping and bushwalking. There's a great village pub, and you can canoe or kayak along the Kangaroo River with

> " If you want a cave experience without the crowds, head 40 minutes north of Lithgow to the Glow Worm Tunnels in Newnes Plateau.

Carlotta Arch, Jenolan Caves

Kangaroo Valley Safaris. Check out the many festivals and markets throughout the year, including the lively Folk Festival every October. Shop for arts and crafts, listen to folk bands from around Australia, and enjoy poetry readings.

Get those legs moving and lace up your hiking boots for a walk along the Griffins Fire Trail in Morton National Park or Cooks Nose in Barren Grounds Nature Reserve.

One hour further south is Jervis Bay National Park, brilliant for scuba diving with weedy seadragons and cuttlefish, dolphin spotting, and walking along the impossibly white sand at Hyams Beach.

The Snowy Mountains

Some of Australia's best ski fields await in the Snowy Mountains in the state's south. Thredbo and Perisher are popular ski resorts, and each year during winter, locals cross their fingers in hope for a good snow season. On the first weekend of winter each year, regardless of the weather, the Snowtunes Music Festival kicks off the coldest season of the year with music, bright lights, and lots of booze.

The Snowys are also a hiking, horse riding, cycling and fishing hotspot in the summer months. While you're in Kosciuszko National Park, hike to the top of mainland Australia's highest peak, Mount Kosciuszko. The 8-mi return (13km) hike isn't too demanding on the knees and offers spectacular views of the mountains and surrounding countryside.

The old mining town of Newcastle

Back on the coast, two hours north of Sydney, the city of Newcastle is the gateway to the Hunter Valley, and is famous for its beautiful surf beaches. Here, nightlife is happening, beaches are quieter, and parking is much easier to find. Take a stroll up to Nobbys Lighthouse, established in 1858, to enjoy coastal views and to learn about the history of the land dating back to the Dreamtime. Take

028

> While you're in Kosciuszko National Park, hike to the top of mainland Australia's highest peak, Mount Kosciuszko.

Byron Bay Lighthouse

beachside camping, fishing, whale watching and swimming in Arakoon National Park before heading north. Dive at Fish Rock with its cave swim-through, and swim among the large schools of fish and many types of subtropical and tropical marine life.

Coffs Harbour

Coffs Harbour, 240mi (540 km) north of Sydney, is dominated by farmland and banana plantations, and the only place in NSW where the Great Dividing Range meets the Pacific Ocean.

Surrounded by national parks and marine reserves, check out nearby Bellingen River and Dorrigo national parks, and take in the view from the mountains to the sea from the Forest Sky Pier at Sealy Lookout.

If you're looking for a challenge, the Yuraygir Coastal Walk, covering 40mi (65km) of coastline, takes four days to complete, and is home to many rare wetland creatures, likes the eastern ground parrot and eastern grass owl.

Go diving offshore from Coffs Harbour to Solitary Islands Marine Park, where the warm tropical waters of the Great Barrier Reef meet the cooler waters from the south. Here, a great mix of tropical and subtropical marine life merge, with colorful corals, sponges and anemones, schools of fish, sharks, turtles, giant cuttlefish, rays, and eels can be seen.

Byron Bay

Chill out in the surf town of Byron Bay

An hour north of Newcastle, Port Stephens is a quiet coastal town with excellent whale watching.

a detour inland to the Hunter Valley to relax with a glass of wine at one of Australia's oldest wineries.

Go sandboarding in Port Stephens

An hour north of Newcastle, Port Stephens is a quiet coastal town with excellent whale watching, May through November, watersports, and fishing. For an adrenaline rush, go sandboarding at Worimi Regional Park (also known as Stockton Sand Dunes) or join a quad biking tour, with a company owned and operated by Indigenous communities.

Barrington Tops and South West Rocks

Venture inland to Barrington Tops National Park, where, during winter, snow falls on the campsites and bushwalking trails. If you've got a 4WD, get the paint dirty on some of the muddy tracks – but don't attempt them without off-road equipment.

Drive east towards the coast again to explore the history of Trial Bay Gaol in South West Rocks, and enjoy while enjoying the waves, nightlife, and food from quirky cafes. It gets busy here, so head south to Ballina to catch the waves at Lighthouse Beach and Lennox Head, or north to beautiful, peaceful Brunswick Heads. Get those limbs moving in the ancient World Heritage-listed rainforests of Nightcap National Park, near Lismore, on the 0.9mi (1.5km) Big Scrub loop walking track.

Go diving at Julian Rocks during summer and autumn to hang out with leopard sharks and manta rays. During the cooler months, grey nurse sharks will arrive. Other marine life include turtles, wobbegongs, eagle rays, starfish, and anemones.

Inland from Byron Bay, check out the busy country towns of Mullumbimby and Bangalow, surrounded by rolling hills, or head northwest to extraordinary Wollumbin National Park.

See Australia's only Dark Sky Park

Venture far into Outback NSW to see the night skies above Warrumbungle National Park. This special place became Australia's only Dark Sky Park because of the exceptional quality of its starry nights, and is also home to Australia's largest optical telescope. This is the perfect spot for star-loving campers. Don't miss the 9mi (14.5km) Breadknife and Grand High Tops walk to see iconic rock formations, wildflowers in spring, and wedge-tailed eagles soaring above in search for prey.

Walls of China, Mungo National Park

Getty Images/mircostov_1

See the Walls of China in Outback NSW

Off the well-driven east coast trail, Mungo National Park is hiding away in the southwest corner of NSW, 625mi (1,006km) or a 15-hour drive from Sydney. This 110,967-hectare national park is rich in Indigenous history. From Mungo lookout, gaze across an ancient ice-age lake bed, where undiscovered bones of original megafauna remain today, and see the iconic Walls of China formation, sculpted over thousands of years by wind and rain. This erosion has revealed artefacts, dating back more than 40,000 years, belonging to the Mutthi Muhhti, Ngyiampaa, and Paakantyi Aboriginal people.

While you're out here, head to the nearby Outback mining town of Broken Hill. The Living Desert Sculptures are a collection of sandstone artworks created by international artists in 1993. Fans of the movie *Mad Max* will enjoy the Mad Max Museum in Silverton, where the movie was filmed. Nearby Mundi Mundi Plains Lookout offers spectacular views of the vast plains.

"
Fans of the movie *Mad Max* will enjoy the Mad Max Museum in Silverton, where the movie was filmed.

Australian Capital Territory

Sydney is often mistaken for the capital of Australia, but 186mi (300km) south, inland from Budawang National Park, is Canberra, in the Australian Capital Territory (ACT).

Canberra

The center of Australia's political life, and the home to many of the country's leading cultural institutions (including the brilliant Australian War Memorial, the National Gallery of Australia, and the National Portrait Gallery), Canberra is often labelled as boring and is accused of having had a fun bypass.

In reality, while the carefully planned capital might seem structured and curated compared to Australia's other cities, Canberra has an exciting food scene, an emerging cool-climate wine

Parliament House, Canberra
Getty Images/Ticoi

region, and is surrounded by pristine countryside. Canberra's growing media industry and a large student population are serviced by hipster markets, cool cafes, festivals and a calendar of events.

Food and nightlife

Head to Lonsdale Street for small bars, industrial cafes and restaurants. Colorful street art and edgy bars make it the ideal place for a night out or slow morning. For something more upscale, Kingston Foreshore is home to restaurants overlooking Lake Burley Griffin, perfect for dinner and with a sunset over the lake. Fyshwick Fresh Food Markets is Canberra's oldest food market and is a great foodie hangout with a fantastic range of seasonal fresh produce, bakery goods, and locally made beer, wine and spirits.

> " Canberra has an exciting food scene, an emerging cool-climate wine region, and is surrounded by pristine countryside.

Getty Images/Garry Hodson
Murrumbidgee river

Canberra

Getty Images/Leeboxjonki

Out of town

More than half of the ACT is a protected nature reserve and national park, with waterfalls, gorges, rives, lookouts, and snow-capped mountains waiting to be explored. There are plenty of walking and mountain biking trails, and places to fish, paddle, climb and camp.

Raft the Murrumbidgee

If grade 3 white-water rapids don't give you dizzy spells of anxiety, book an exhilarating whitewater adventure just outside Canberra. From July to December, day trips can be booked through Alpine River Adventures. Before you book, check to make sure your travel insurance policy covers this activity.

Strap on the hiking boots

Tidbinbilla Nature Reserve, is a 40-minute drive from Canberra, and a great place for hiking. Here you'll spot kangaroos, koalas, possums, emus and, possibly, even a platypus. At the northern end of the Australian Alps, Namadgi National Park has mountain biking trails, horse riding and the Bendora Arboretum heritage track, which passes through a conifer forest.

Walk part of the 90mi (145km) Centenary Trail which takes in all of Canberra in a loop following the NSW border, tackle the well-signposted 16mi (27km) Murrumbidgee Discovery Track that crosses the cliffs of Red Rock Gorge (and take a dip in the Kambah Pools swimming hole while you're there), or take a 2.7mi (4.5km) return hike to the top of Mt Ainslie that rises up behind the Australian War Memorial.

> " Here you'll spot kangaroos, koalas, possums, emus and, possibly, even a platypus.

Victoria

Melbourne is a vibrant, multicultural city, but there is a lot more to Victoria than its bustling capital. If you're road-tripping your way around Victoria, you'll be rewarded with stunning landscapes, historic towns, and abundant wildlife.

Mt Hotham in Winter

Getty Images/FiledIMAGE

Walking with wildlife in Gippsland

Gippsland is a highlight of southeast Victoria. Wilsons Promontory (known as The Prom) is one of the state's best-loved national parks, with turquoise waters, white sand beaches, sand dunes and temperate rainforests. The hiking here is spectacular, and there are more than 49mi (80km) of walking tracks. Test your stamina on the 11.8mi (19km) walk from Telegraph Saddle to the lighthouse – the southernmost occupied point of mainland Australia. Along the way, you'll see eastern grey kangaroos, swamp wallabies, emus, wombats, and fairy-wrens.

The natural beauty of Gippsland is on full show in Croajingolong National Park, one of 12 World Biosphere Reserves in Australia. Koalas hide in the gum trees along the path of the Double Creek Nature Walk, and kangaroos graze near the banks of the Mallacoota Inlet.

Adventure in the Victorian High Country

The High Country in northeast Victoria is where you'll find the state's highest mountains, snowfields, vineyards, and a colorful history. Learn about the notorious bushrangers (outlaws who lived in the bush and were widespread in this area in the 1850s) in the town of Glenrowan, where you can visit the Ned Kelly Museum and Homestead. Follow the interpretive displays to find out more about Australia's most famous bushranger.

Visit the towns of Bright and Myrtleford in fall (March, April and May), when leaves turn red, amber and orange. As winter rolls in, keen snowboarders and skiers migrate to Mount Buller, Mount Buffalo, Mount Hotham, and Falls Creek. Once the snow melts, bushwalkers, horse riders, and cyclists come out in force, ready to tackle the tracks.

Most of the trails throughout the High Country are shared among

> "
> As winter rolls in, keen snowboarders and skiers migrate to Mount Buller, Mount Buffalo, Mount Hotham, and Falls Creek.

033

Loch Ard Gorge

Getty Images/AFR

> Starting
> in Port
> Campbell,
> drive the
> iconic 86mi
> (140km)
> loop of the
> 12 Apostles
> Gourmet Trail.

walkers, runners and riders, and the most popular paths are the 1.9mi (3.1km) Family Trail starting at the clocktower in the Mt Buller village square, the 2.4mi (4km) Mt Timbertop walk located on Howqua Track just past Merrijig, and the 2.7mi (4.5km) Packhorse Heritage Trail starting from Falls Creek village.

Food, wine and whiskey

Starting in Port Campbell, drive the iconic 86mi (140km) loop of the 12 Apostles Gourmet Trail, which takes in local farmers selling gourmet cheese, ice cream, whiskey, olives, chocolate, snails (yep, snails), strawberries, wine, beer and fudge.

Check out great wineries in the High Country, including Feathertop and Gapsted. In May each year, the High Country Harvest Festival celebrates local food, wine and craft beer. Or, if single malt whiskey is more your flavor, visit the Whiskery

in Drysdale, which also offers home made gin.

An easy 90 minutes east of Melbourne, the Yarra Valley is a thriving wine region. Take your time checking out the cellar (and distillery) doors including Four Pillars, a boutique gin distillery that uses Australian native botanicals, and TarraWarra Estate, offering wine and spectacular views.

Hanging Rock

Venture out to Hanging Rock in central Victoria, and stop by the Hanging Rock Discovery Centre to learn how Indigenous Australians used the area for more than 26,000 years, the geology of the unusual volcanic formation, and the background to Joan Lindsay's famous book, *Picnic at Hanging Rock*. Take a walk on the trails to see this volcanic plug that has been exposed to the elements, causing erosion and resulting in very unusual landscapes. Pack your camping gear to spend a few days exploring the Macedon Ranges.

Take a step back in time

Drive north of Melbourne to the gold rush town of Bendigo to see the thriving arts scene and gilded history, then continue north to Echuca on the banks of the Murray River, where the whistles of paddle steamers fill the air as you cruise down the river, passing ancient river gums and imagining what the area was like in the 1800s when this was one of Victoria's busiest stretches of water for trading wool from nearby sheep stations.

Grampians National Park

Getty Images/John Crux Photography

Rock art and nature in The Grampians

The Grampians, or Gariwerd as it is traditionally known, has been central to the dreaming of Aboriginal people for more than 30,000 years. It's home to more than 80% of Victoria's rock art sites, and other ancient Indigenous artifacts such as stones for tool making and oven. Go hiking, camping, mountain biking, fishing, see waterfalls, or try abseiling and rock climbing (check your travel insurance policy to be sure you're covered for these activities).

From Melbourne, take the Western Highway to Halls Gap, traveling through Beaufort. On your way, stop off at Michael Unwin and Mt Langi Ghiran vineyards to sample some fine shiraz. The Brambuk Center in Halls Gap is a great place to learn about the significance of the Grampians for Indigenous people, where Aboriginal guides offer tours to rock art sites.

There are a number of spectacular waterfalls in the Grampians National Park, including the powerful 115ft (35m) high MacKenzie Falls. Swimming isn't allowed, so locals head to the deep pools of Fish Falls for a dip, which is near Zumsteins picnic area. Take the easy or medium trail to The Pinnacle Lookout, a 3.4-mile (5.5km) round trip from the Wonderland carpark, offering spectacular views of the eastern Grampians.

The Mornington Peninsula

An hour southeast of Melbourne, the Mornington Peninsula has a stunning coastline, abundant marine life, vibrant coastal villages, and delicious local food and wine.

The charming towns of Flinders and Balnarring are a great place to

> " The Grampians, or Gariwerd as it is traditionally known, has been central to the dreaming of Aboriginal people for more than 30,000 years.

Brighton Beach

Island, a two-hour drive southeast of Melbourne, to see the Penguin Parade at Summerland Beach. Spectators must stay a safe distance away while they watch, every night at dusk, hundreds of small penguins emerge nervously from the ocean to make their way up the beach to their burrows for the night. Adorable.

Take a day trip to Phillip Island, a two-hour drive southeast of Melbourne, to see the Penguin Parade at Summerland Beach.

stop off for a meal in a cozy pub.

The rugged and historic Cape Schanck Lighthouse Reserve, in Mornington Peninsula National Park, has spectacular wild beaches and rugged basalt cliffs. Take a walk along the Bushrangers Bay Walking Track for views over the pristine coastline and, further along the coast, you can soak in healing thermal waters at the Peninsula Hot Springs or don a mask and snorkel to spot sea dragons under Rye Pier.

Dandenong Ranges National Park

The winding roads of Dandenong Ranges National Park, just one hour from Melbourne, are riddled with quaint villages and artists' studios, and forests of mountain ash and fern gullies. Walk or run up the 1,000 steps, a 1.8mi (3km) track ascending through a damp fern valley up through tree ferns and manna gums.

Go surfing in Torquay

Catch a wave at Torquay's beaches, which are surrounded by high cliffs forming a natural amphitheater. The golden sand and rolling swells are just over an hour from Melbourne, so there's plenty of time to surf and visit the world's largest surfing/beach culture museum, the Australian National Surfing Museum.

Phillip Island

There are few things cuter than seeing tiny penguins in their natural habitat. Take a day trip to Phillip

The Pinnacles Rock, Phillip Island

Tasmania

Once the butt of jokes by its mainland cousins, Tasmania is now a go-to destination with cool festivals headlined by international acts, historic cinemas with a modern twist and public nudity that is legal once a year.

Cradle Mountain

Megan Jerrard

Then vs now

A decade or two ago, there were two places your parents or grandparents would go for a holiday, either a wine tour in South Australia or an RV trip around Tasmania in true 'grey nomad' style.

Fast forward to now, and travel in Tasmania is booming. What was once a state that only came alive in summer with the finish of the iconic Sydney to Hobart Yacht Race, now boasts a year-round calendar of broad ranging events, attracting everyone from hipsters, backpackers, foodies and anyone else who feels left out at dinner parties because they haven't been to MONA.

The MONA effect

This is the term locals use to explain the explosion of interest in the island state. In fact, the founder of the Museum of Old and New Art (MONA) David Walsh, a long-haired arts patron from the working-class northern suburbs of Hobart, is often referred to as Tasmania's unofficial leader.

MONA is responsible for the summer festival MONA FOMA, curated by Violent Femmes guitarist Brian Ritchie. Using his industry contacts, a state that once struggled to lure any big-name acts can now boast the likes of The Flaming Lips, Gotye, Philip Glass and Nick Cave in its past line-ups.

While once Tasmanians hibernated during the bitterly cold and long winter, another brainchild of Walsh, Dark MOFO has lured them out of their homes, alongside thousands of interstate and international visitors, to celebrate the Southern Hemisphere's winter solstice with musical acts, art installations, food, artisan beers and spirits. The festival wraps up with a nude swim, where shrinkage is guaranteed as the temperature struggles to get into double figures in the early morning.

And Walsh hasn't stopped there; stay tuned for his hotel and casino, HoMo.

> " What was once a state that only came alive in summer with the finish of the iconic Sydney to Hobart Yacht Race, now boasts a year-round calendar of broad ranging events.

Hartz Mountains National Park

Getty Images/Posnov

> Tasmanians are fiercely loyal, so it's often a surprise to visitors that people in the north are not huge fans of the south and vice versa.

On the road

If you want to escape the crowds, but still love getting amongst the vibe, get yourself to Golconda in the state's remote northeast. For two nights and three days in March, the 50-acre private property opens its gates for the Panama Festival. Don't be fooled by the name, you won't find a bush band banging a Mendoza on the main stage.

Nearby, but later in the year, the North East Rivers Festival kicks off, an event that started with a single river race 40 years ago. If you don't mind getting wet and covered in flour bombs, enter a homemade raft or boat in the Derby River Derby and tackle the rapids of the Ringarooma River. The festival is now so popular it's expanded from that race to two full weekends of action.

And if you are traveling to Golconda from Hobart, make sure you stop at Elephant Pass and enjoy a stack of pancakes overlooking the Tasman Sea.

A state divided

Tasmanians are fiercely loyal, so it's often a surprise to visitors that people in the north are not huge fans of the south and vice versa. Whether you are from Hobart or Launceston, the state's two biggest cities, each argue the best thing about the others' respective cities is the view in the rear-vision mirror as they drive away.

The rivalry even extends to which beer you drink. Take a tour of James Boags Brewery in Launceston but don't mention the 'c' word. Cascade is the beer brewed in the south of the state. While both breweries are rich in history, a bloke at a pub in Hobart would never order a beer brewed in Launceston. You be the judge.

If beer is not your thing, visit Willie Smith's Apple Shed in the Huon, south of Hobart, for a cider. It ticks all the boxes, it's organic, served in a rustic barn with Sunday sessions and quality produce. The nearby museum tells the story behind the orchard industry's comeback in the region, helping the state reclaim the title of the 'Apple Isle'.

Tassie's deep south

Further south in the Huon, the tiny town of Geeveston is where you'll find the best sushi in the state at Masaaki's Sushi. But you need to be quick, chef Masaaki Koyoma only opens on weekends, is sold out by mid-afternoon and closes early Sunday to go surfing.

While in Geeveston, you can explore the Hartz Mountains, Huon and Picton Rivers, Hastings Caves and relax in the thermal springs.

When you get back to Huonville, return to Hobart via Cygnet. It's popular among people desiring an alternative lifestyle and is full of art studios and galleries. It's also where renowned former *Sydney Morning Herald* restaurant critic Matthew Evans first lived when he moved to Tasmania. His story, documented in the TV series *Gourmet Farmer*, has been credited with luring people to Tassie from around the world looking for a 'food change'.

A good old-fashioned movie house

In Hobart, the State Cinema is the place to go. It screens arthouse and foreign movies alongside blockbusters. Find out what's being screened in cinema five or eight and you will enjoy an intimate experience with just a few leather couches surrounded by sandstone walls. Make sure you grab a glass of Tassie

Getty Images/janettaasche

Walk the Three Capes Track

Standing on Australia's tallest sea cliffs, towering 984ft (300m) over the Southern Ocean, can be vertigo-inducing, but their raw beauty is worth the challenge. The track passes a fabled rock climbing route, The Totem Pole, along with eucalypt forests, heaths and moors and the pristine sands of Fortescue Bay. Camping sites must be booked in advance for this circular walk, and include a bed in comfortable hiker cabins, a boat cruise to the trailhead, and a bus back to the start.

Time: 28mi/46km, four days

Getting there: Catch a bus 1.5 hrs from Hobart to Port Arthur.

Tip: With a bed and cooking facilities provided, you'll have more space to pack a bottle of wine.

Difficulty: Moderate

Many of Tassie's multi-day hikes require thorough planning. Advanced bookings and permits may be required, and there are restrictions such as daily limits on the number of hikers allowed, as well as areas that are off-limits to trekkers.

red. The cinema is at the top of the restaurant strip in North Hobart.

The art-deco Star Theatre in Launceston is another independent cinema screening fewer mainstream films. Like the State Cinema, it has a bar and café with relaxed seating options.

A protected island

More than 40% of Tasmania is a national park, reserve, or conservation area. At the heart of Tasmania's conservation efforts is the Tasmanian Wilderness World Heritage Area, which covers nearly 20% of the island. Tasmania has 19 national parks, more than 400 conservation areas, and hundreds of nature reserves and historic sites.

While Cradle Mountain - Lake St Clair National Park receives the most attention, due to its modern facilities, popular Dove Lake Circuit Trail, and the world-famous Overland Track, it is the lesser-known parks and reserves which offer pure wilderness.

Find Aboriginal heritage sites, shipwrecks and lighthouses in Rocky Cape National Park, or go camping among iconic animals such as Tasmanian devils, wombats, pademelons and sea eagles in Narawntapu National Park. Take a short hike around the park's Springlawn Lagoon in the early morning for your best chance of spotting wildlife.

National parks, such as Freycinet, offer well-groomed, sign-posted trails that take you to beautiful sights, including Wineglass Bay. A visit to Southwest National Park will require careful planning, as much of this national park is unexplored, and is home to rare animals such as the critically endangered orange-bellied parrot. Some areas of the park can be accessed by road, but others, such as the South Coast Track, require a helicopter to enter, before you hike out.

Go diving at Cathedral Cave
Australia's largest sea cave, Cathedral

Tarkine

Megan Jerrard

Cave, welcomes divers through its massive opening, leading into a maze of caverns and passages. Access to this site is weather-dependent, so check with your dive operator. Marine life includes weedy seadragons, turtles, fish, cuttlefish, plus smaller marine animals such as nudibranchs and sea spiders.

Take a drive to Port Arthur
Take a drive from Hobart to the historic convict settlement turned open-air museum at Port Arthur. Walking through the remnants of the buildings, you can almost hear the cries and despair of the convicts that were imprisoned here with no hope of escape. On the way to Port Arthur, stop off to see the natural rock formations of the Devil's Kitchen, the Tessellated Pavement, and Tasman Arch.

Tarkine Forest Reserve
Get lost in the prehistoric-looking Tarkine Forest Reserve, home to Australia's largest temperate

Get lost in the prehistoric-looking Tarkine Forest Reserve, home to Australia's largest temperate rainforest.

rainforest. The Tarkine Drive circuit cuts through Tasmania's northwest, and is dotted with numerous hiking trails and camping areas along the coast and deeper into the rainforest.

Bay of Fires

Take the Great Eastern Drive
White sand beaches and crystal-clear waters can be found on the Great Eastern Drive, guiding you from the scenic Bay of Fires to Orford. Further south along the coast, take a hike for a better chance of seeing wildlife in Freycinet and Maria Island National Park.

Chase a waterfall, or three
The only thing better than witnessing the roar of a waterfall is not having to share the experience with anyone else. Across Tasmania, countless waterfalls can be accessed via a short hike that'll bring you close enough to feel the cool mist on your face. The rainy winter season brings many of the falls to life, including the elegant Liffey Falls and the towering Montezuma Falls, Tasmania's tallest. Seek out rare, quiet spots like Lobster Falls or Redwater Creek Falls, which rarely see visitors for weeks at a time.

Some of Australia's longest and deepest cave systems
Mole Creek Caves in Tasmania's north are home to entrancing glow worms, stalactites, stalagmites, and shimmering crystals. If you are a bit claustrophobic, instead head south of Hobart to the spacious Hastings Caves where you'll also find a thermal pool to soothe the legs after climbing the cave's many stairs.

Don't miss Tassie's offshore islands
Travel back in time with a visit to Maria Island, which was once home to convict settlements but now provides a safe refuge for wildlife, including introduced devils. Search for albino wallabies on Bruny Island, dine on fresh seafood on King Island, and escape modern life on Flinders Island.

> " White sand beaches and crystal-clear waters can be found on the Great Eastern Drive.

Port Arthur

041

Queensland

There's more to Queensland than the Great Barrier Reef, with ancient rainforests, epic four-wheel driving tracks, exciting islands, national parks and Outback pubs.

Daintree Rainforest

From Cairns, head north (by car, bus, seaplane or helicopter) to explore the Daintree National Park, a spectacularly green and wild environment that teems with life.

The Daintree, with its dense tropical foliage, huge fan palms, big crocodiles and tiny tree frogs, is a UNESCO World Heritage site, and is the oldest, continuously surviving tropical rainforest on earth, estimated to be 165 million years old. Yikes!

Head to Cape Tribulation, the remote, desolate beach edged by mangroves (explore those via the boardwalk). It's known for its windswept beach reminiscent of a desert island. Always read the signs, and if it says not to swim, don't swim.

The Daintree River is home to a number of large saltwater crocodiles, which are a must-see (from afar). Take a crocodile boat cruise to spot the prehistoric critters that make North Queensland their playground.

Another fascinating, and dangerous, inhabitant of northern Queensland is the cassowary, a very large, shy but aggressive bird, found in the Paluma Range National Park.

Cape Tribulation

Getty Images/Darren Tierney

Day trips from Cairns

Take a one hour drive inland from Cairns to see the Atherton Tablelands. Visit the huge Cathedral and Curtain fig trees, and camp on the shores of Lake Tinaroo.

Take a short drive to Kuranda to see the mighty waterfalls in Barron Gorge National Park. After heavy rain, the power of the waterfalls is a sight to behold, whether that be as a passenger on board the heritage railway, or while taking a stroll along the boardwalk from the car park to see them from afar.

Two hours south of Cairns, see the iconic Millaa Millaa Falls. Surrounded by rainforest, the falls cascade into a waterhole where you can enjoy a refreshing dip.

Closer to town, take a drive to Stoney Creek Falls, a series of cascading waterfalls with a short uphill walking trail. You could take

> **66**
>
> The Daintree, with its dense tropical foliage, huge fan palms, big crocodiles and tiny tree frogs, is a UNESCO World Heritage site.

a swim, but always ask the locals before putting your little toes into the water, as Tropical North Queensland is crocodile country.

Magnetic Island

Take a 20-minute ferry ride from Townsville across Cleveland Bay to 'Maggie', where 2,000 people make this magnificent island their home. More than two-thirds of the island is a national park, with boulder-strewn headlands, hoop pines, sandy beaches and fringing coral reefs. Composed mostly of granite, Magnetic Island was once part of the mainland before the sea level rose about 7,500 years ago.

Rent a convertible or a classic moke and explore Mt Cook, the highest point on the island (named after Captain Cook who discovered the island and believed it affected his compass), or head to one of the island's fantastic fishing spots.

Do the Forts Walk from Bungalow Bay Koala Village to spot one of the island's 800+ wild koalas. You can also climb concrete structures from the Second World War for panoramic views of the island.

Laze on the beach at Horseshoe Bay, and sit on the jetty at Picnic Bay as the sun sets over the sea.

Paluma Range National Park

Find Big and Little Crystal Creek in Paluma Range National Park, two lucky finds in the far north. After following a steep, winding road into the hills, you'll be rewarded with a series of swimmable waterfalls and deep pools at Little Crystal Creek. A historic bridge spans the creek, and just below it is a popular rock face used as a diving board, but always check the water levels before taking the plunge. Find natural rock slides and the swimming hole known as the Paradise Pool at Big Crystal Creek.

Set up camp at Crystal Creek campsite, where large shaded areas give you the chance to relax beneath the rainforest or walk one of a number of short trails surrounding the site. Wake up early to take a morning dip in the nearby waterhole before cooking up some breakfast over your campfire.

Go diving at Lady Elliot Island

At the southern end of the Great

> Laze on the beach at Horseshoe Bay, and sit on the jetty at Picnic Bay as the sun sets over the sea.

Magnetic Island

Pixabay/bongkochflame

Barrier Reef, between Fraser and Lady Musgrave Islands, Lady Elliot was declared a No-Take fishing zone in 2005, and has become one of the most biodiverse spots on the Great Barrier Reef. Tiny marine critters and big ocean giants (such as manta rays, turtles and at the right time of year, whales) call it home.

This is one of the best spots on the reef to see giant manta rays and several species of turtle all year around. Plus, a large variety of fish species, corals, clams, starfish and many other small marine creatures which call the many bommies, caves, and reefs home. The wreck of the *Severance*, sunk in 1999, is the place to see colorful fish and occasional ray visitors.

Road to Birdsville
Jo Stewart

Find a platypus in Finch Hatton Gorge

You might strike luck in Finch Hatton Gorge, where many platypus call the forests and waterways home. These diminutive, and notoriously shy mammals are hard to spot, but for the lucky few who get to see them in the wild, the memory will last a lifetime. If you've packed camping gear, spend a night in the wilderness at Platypus Bush Camp, and hikers should take the Wheel of Fire Walk, keeping an eye out for the large groups of fruit bats which call the forest home.

Discover Queensland's Outback

Queensland isn't all beaches and rainforests (although, to be fair, a lot of it is). Travel southwest from Townsville toward Charters Towers, to Ravenswood, a small historic mining town in the Queensland Outback. History buffs will love the Ravenswood Railway Hotel, a heritage landmark retaining original furniture, rooms, and fittings. It's said to be haunted, so if you're brave enough, you can stay the night. If you don't fancy a night in the hotel, there's a campground nearby, so pack your camping gear in case you chicken out.

Drive further west into the Outback along the Flinders Highway to Mount Isa, a mining town 570mi (917km) west from Townsville. Fans of Western films should check out the annual Mount Isa Rodeo held in early August, or join a tour to learn about some of the mines in town. If a bit of WWII history interests you, check out the underground hospital.

Queensland's 4WD island escapes

World Heritage-listed Fraser Island lies off the coast of Queensland,

66
You might strike luck in Finch Hatton Gorge, where many platypus call the forests and waterways home.

near Hervey Bay, just north of the Sunshine Coast. It's the world's largest sand island, and Seventy Five Mile Beach is an official highway with a speed limit of 49mi/hr (80km/hr), while the inland roads have a limit of 21mi/hr (35km/hr). Driving conditions vary with the tide and weather, but normal road rules apply. Seventy-Five Mile Beach is also one of the best beach fishing locations in the world. The interior of Fraser is covered by rainforest, with beautiful freshwater lakes including Lake McKenzie and vivid green Lake Wabby, surrounded by sand dunes.

Take a dip in the Champagne Pools, as the water from the ocean crashes against the rocks, and look out for the abundance of wildlife, including 47 species of mammals, more than 354 species of birds and 79 species of reptiles. Accommodation on Fraser Island ranges from luxury to budget, and is a great place to camp with several campgrounds where you can cook your own meals, set up tents and

Outback Pubs in Queensland

Birdsville Hotel

On the edge of the Simpson Desert, in a remote corner of Outback Queensland, the Birdsville Hotel has welcomed travelers since 1884. A place that revels in its legendary status as a pub that has endured the highest recorded temperature in Queensland (a sizzling 121.1°F / 49.5°C), here you can expect to encounter leather-clad bikers, caked in red dust, alongside well-dressed retirees ticking another Outback pub off their list. In the Front Bar, an eclectic mishmash of memorabilia catalogues the pub's history of attracting explorers, wayfarers, wanderers, rovers and larrikins, with the Hat Wall paying tribute to long serving Birdsville locals. Grab a beer, sit on the veranda and watch small planes take off from the airport across from the pub. There's no airport bar like it anywhere else in the world!

Betoota Pub

Driving in Queensland's Diamantina Shire means traveling on long, bumpy stretches of unsealed road with nothing on the horizon but red earth, feral cattle and the odd dead tree. That is, until you reach the ghost town of Betoota. Once a busy outpost, Betoota's population plunged to zero after the death of the local publican in 2004. You won't be able to get a beer, but an obligatory stop at the creepy, abandoned Betoota pub is a must in a place with few other options to break up the trip. Stand at the eerily silent bar, close your eyes and listen for the clinking glasses of the ghosts of drinkers past.

Lions Den Hotel

With walls plastered with bumper stickers, memorabilia, newspaper articles and graffiti, this long-standing Far North Queensland roadhouse serves beer and pizza with a side serve of dry Australian humor. A magnet for travelers drawn to the region for fishing, camping and off-roading, this is the type of place you'll hear laconic drinkers spinning tall tales of miraculous escapes from giant crocodiles and epic battles with the one that got away.

Western Star Hotel

In Queensland's Channel Country, the blink-and-you'll-miss-it town of Windorah is a popular stopping point for travelers driving to Birdsville from Longreach, Charleville and beyond. Windorah's Western Star Hotel has all the hallmarks of a good bush pub with wood-paneled interiors, ceiling fans circulating in tempo, XXXX brand beer and a dart board that has seen better days. There is nothing more True Blue Aussie than sitting on a pub veranda, with a beer in hand, as flocks of cockatoos fly overhead.

Getty Images/tmpuevokeonardo

Fraser Island

camp out under the stars.

If Fraser Island isn't offering the isolation you're looking for, take a 75-minute ferry ride from Brisbane to Moreton Island. Get around by 4WD to explore the lakes, lagoons, and three heritage sites. Go whale or dolphin watching, diving or snorkeling, explore Moreton Island National Park, join a 4WD tour, or experience the thrill of sand tobogganing.

Mt Ngungun, Glass House Mountains

Getty Images/Posnov

The Glass House Mountains

Get up high on a hike up Mount Beerwah which can be summited via a mile-long (2.6km) trail. The hike can be dangerous with steep banks and uneven ground, so take care on the way up. If you're not keen on the climb, a fine lookout over the mountains can be found along the Glass House Woodford Road.

Just outside of the park, Mount Ngungun can also be summited via a similarly demanding track. There are a number of shorter walks and trails along with picnic spots to soak in the afternoon sun or spot lazy koalas. Another great spot to view the mountains is McCarthy's Lookout, just south of Maleny.

Springbrook National Park

On the border of Queensland and New South Wales, Springbrook National Park is very different from the far north, with forests of fungi, moss and thick foliage that flourish among the damp and often misty mountains.

If the weather is clear you'll be in luck, so take a short walk through the beech forest for views from Best of All Lookout. Head to Canyon Lookout from where you can access several short and longer trails, and don't miss the natural bridge at Cave Creek before walking one of the trails nearby.

Lamington National Park

Close to Springbrook, and part of the Gondwana Rainforest, the road connecting Lamington and Springbrook National Park is a steep, windy but beautiful 90-minute drive. The Green Mountains campsite is inside the national park, and access to the Python Rock lookout, Moonlight Crag and the Morans Falls walk is easy after the long hairpin drive up. There are more than 93mi (150km) of walking tracks in the park, including the 33mi (54km) Gold Coast Hinterland Great Walk, which can be started from the campsite.

> " There are a number of shorter walks and trails along with picnic spots to soak in the afternoon sun or spot lazy koalas.

Jennifer Neal

A Rap Battle With Snakes on Walsh's Pyramid

An outdoor not-so-enthusiast tackles one of Australia's most unforgiving hikes.

" Wait, are there snakes on this mountain, ya think?" I asked my friend over the phone, who had graciously volunteered to accompany me – by phone, at least – on the first few steps of my hike. I hate snakes.

"Good chance," he replied. "But you know, just stomp your feet, clap your hands and sing to give them some warning of your whereabouts, so they can scamper off, and you'll be fine."

"I don't know what to sing," I said.

"Well, then rap," he responded.

We hung up and I faced the dry, barren brush of Walsh's Pyramid on my own. A thinly defined path lay before me, covered in layers of crunchy brown bush and long, dried sticks from which various creatures darted in and out. Hawks circled overhead, and kookaburras guffawed from the surrounding shrubbery.

It was only a 3,097ft (922m) hike to the summit, but a near-vertical climb that would challenge even the most experienced bushwalker...or, in my case, body pumper.

"I like big butts and I cannot lie..." I started singing, while clapping my hands half-heartedly, and stomping my feet as loudly as I could. I headed up the trail one step at a time, with Sir Mix-a-Lot as company.

Up until then, the most challenging feat of athleticism I had faced was managing to make it to a gym class three days a week. I had always shied

Jennifer Neal

Jennifer is a journalist, author, stand-up comedian, and visual artist who writes about intersections of race, sexuality, gender and migration.

away from physical tasks that required long-term commitment and unavoidable amounts of pain. In body pump, the weights could be adjusted, and 45 minutes of high-interval training would be followed by a nice, relaxing stretch that made me feel good about myself again before meeting up with girlfriends to eat pizza.

But Les Mills' full-body weights and cardio workout never required knowledge of rough, jagged terrain, inland taipans (the world's most venomous snake), or any number of bushwalking survival hacks that I should have studied before tackling one of Australia's most unforgiving hikes.

> " I might have known to wear actual hiking boots, instead of Nike trainers with white rubber soles.

If they had, I might have known to wear actual hiking boots, instead of Nike trainers with white rubber soles. Or long-sleeved attire that would protect me from the brutal sun (and possible snake bites), instead of the fast-wicking apparel I usually reserved for my gym class. I also might have paced myself a little better for a hike that takes experienced bushwalkers between three and four hours to ascend, but took me six and a half.

Pilates didn't prepare me for that. Body balance didn't prepare me for that. No amount of squats in the world prepared me for that.

A short drive south of Cairns, Walsh's Pyramid is an intimidating structure – not the least of which because it's the highest freestanding pyramid in the world. Coated in sparse vegetation that bakes beneath the tropical Queensland sun, there's little to provide shelter for its vast array of slithery inhabitants – snakes, geckos, and me.

After having found Nemo on the Great Barrier Reef and eaten my way through a series of food-related tourist traps in the Daintree Rainforest, I was ready for a new challenge – one that nearly killed me.

Because I was hiking alone (which I don't recommend for inexperienced climbers or basically anyone smarter than me), I had to devise ways to keep myself psychologically engaged. Besides rapping, I picked leaves and created origami concoctions while stopping for water breaks. I finished week-old arguments with colleagues while fashioning a hiking stick with my pocketknife. I meditated on the possibility of a Trump presidency while playfully chasing geckos (my only hiking companions) on trees that hung a bit too close to the edge of a cliff.

A NOMAD'S STORY

I snaked up the mountain rock by gigantic rock, using muscles I had never felt before, bracing myself as close to the steep slopes as I could. When I was forced to climb an intimidating boulder by gripping, pushing, and sliding over a rough, hot stone-surface that terrified me with its girth – I realized I may have gotten a little over my head.

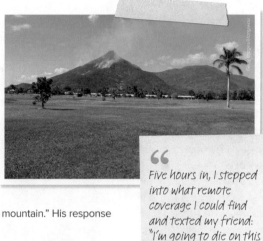

Five hours in, I stepped into what remote coverage I could find and texted my friend: "I'm going to die on this mountain." His response was swift and mocking: "Quitter."

Damn right, I thought.

> **"** Five hours in, I stepped into what remote coverage I could find and texted my friend: "I'm going to die on this mountain."

Having peed a suspicious brown urine over what felt like the edge of the world, I pushed the impending threat of more serious (say, kidney-related) health ailments out of my head and sat down for what I thought would be the end of my hike. Right then, another hiker – the only one I'd seen all day – approached from behind with the steam of a freight train. She was a Maori woman with ropey muscles that hoisted her up the Pyramid at double my speed. She stopped and asked me if I was all right. "Oh, I don't know. Maybe?" I replied.

After a failed attempt to tandem together, I let her go ahead of me, huffing and puffing in her direction until her hot pink singlet disappeared from view. As she descended, seemingly minutes later, she told me I was really close, and not to give up. Then she gave me two handfuls of gummy snakes, a pear, and an apple and wished me well before heading back down the mountain.

To this day, I don't know who that woman was, but I do believe she was single-handedly responsible for ensuring that I didn't end up on the five o'clock news.

I inhaled the snakes, which tasted to my depleted senses like they had a touch of the divine. Their sugar propelled me toward the top of the summit, where I emptied my camel pack and ate the fruit all the way down to the seeds as, below me, the clouds started rolling in and the sun sank towards the horizon.

Shaking, sore, and ecstatic, I texted my friend photos from the summit. He replied "Oh, so you're not a quitter then, hey?"

Jerk.

I used to think hiking was for daredevils and adrenaline junkies who don't appreciate the subtle nuance of staying home and doing nothing. Or the kinds of people who believe that a brush with death is akin to an appreciation for life – like people who swim with great white sharks. But as I stood on top of this rock looking down at the world, I felt like I had conquered something that didn't belong to me – a piece of a world that shows no mercy to her inhabitants. But more than that, I had conquered my fears of physical exertion outside of the parameters of a group class, and pushed myself to the edge of my endurance.

My reward was a view of such grandeur that I tried to memorize every detail – every rolling hill, every shadow cast by a hovering cloud, and every patch of farmland meticulously segregated in an impressive geometric display.

Australia was showing off with her beauty that day, and I felt like I was the recipient of a private show-and-tell that left me breathless.

"I conquered you!" I screamed from the top of the rock. The wind responded with the smell of rain.

> **"**
> My reward was a view of such grandeur that I tried to memorize every detail – every rolling hill, every shadow cast by a hovering cloud.

But I hadn't conquered the steady descent. My wobbly legs buckled halfway down and I rolled my ankle, releasing a blood-curdling scream that sent every kookaburra on the Pyramid into a laughing fit. I spent two hours crawling through the brush, unsure of what I would uncover with each handful of dried leaves, crying to no one and long overdue for my celebratory dinner of fish and chips. It should have put me off hiking forever, but it had the opposite effect.

I've often mocked people for attempting to vanquish nature, because nature always has the last word in the end. But I understand now that it's not about subduing; it's about submitting. In order to make it up that mountain and back, I had to submit to my fears and re-emerge humbled but stronger.

"...you other brothers can't deny..."

I started rapping all over again, pulling myself inch by inch closer to my rental car.

"That when a girl walks by with an itty-bitty waist, and a round thing in your face, you get sprung."

Getty Images - Whitworth Images

OUTBACK & CENTRAL AUSTRALIA

Endless miles of driving along red dirt roads will require patience, not to mention a lot of preparation, but where else in the world can you see kangaroos bounce across sparse Outback landscapes, or experience a rich Aboriginal culture? So, head out of the cities for adventures in the desert and beyond.

South Australia

South Australia has long been underrated by travelers, but take a journey from the Great Australian Bight to the Outback, and you'll soon see why this is one of Australia's best adventure destinations.

Kangaroo Island

Belair National Park

Established in 1891, Belair is the state's oldest national park, and is only a half hour drive from Adelaide, making for an easy day trip if you don't have time to explore further.

Take a hike through the park to see fire scars on ancient trees, Indigenous tree carvings, waterfalls, lakes and wildflowers. There are several scenic picnic spots including at Long Gully and on the shore of Playford Lake. For travelers with families, try Wood Duck Walk, a 0.6mi (1km) circuit that takes about half an hour, where you can see (you guessed it) ducks!

If you're an experienced hiker, head for the Adventure Loop Trail, a steep 7.8mi (12.6km), six-hour hike that circles around the whole national park. Or swap out your hiking boots for two wheels and take on the path with a mountain bike.

The wine state

The Barossa Valley, an hour from Adelaide, is one of the oldest and most acclaimed wine regions in the world. Channel your inner sommelier at one of the wine schools in the area to learn about the intricate differences in tastes and textures. If you'd rather be drinking that learning, you can visit two of the most famous wineries, Penfolds or Rockford, on a wine tasting tour.

In Clare Valley, two hours from Adelaide, Claymore Wines has a great selection of locally produced wines, as well as cheeses and olives to keep your stomach full during a day at the vineyard.

Eden Valley is another wine region just over an hour's drive from Adelaide. The region is known for its great Riesling and Shiraz, due to the perfect climate. At Flaxman or Fernfield Wines tuck into great wine and local food, such as the broad selection of cheese platters or Mt Pleasant smoked salmon tartlets.

> The Barossa Valley, an hour from Adelaide, is one of the oldest and most acclaimed wine regions in the world.

Barossa Valley vineyard

Getty Images/Heciellis

Drive the Eyre Peninsula Seafood Trail

South Australia is known for its abundance of seafood, and the local seafood industry places a major focus on freshness and sustainability.

Follow the Eyre Peninsula Seafood Trail between Whyalla and Ceduna; along the way, try fresh prawns, oysters, lobsters, tuna, and more. Stop at Tumba Bay and have a go at catching your own lunch on a chartered fishing tour searching for King George whiting. Locks Well, between Port Lincoln and Streaky Bay, is known as one of the best salmon fishing spots in Australia, and there is an abundance of quality salmon in restaurants in the area.

On the road

Start your road trip in the far southeastern corner of the state at Mount Gambier, and explore the 90ft-deep cave in Cave Gardens, or take a guided tour of the sinkhole cave system at Engelbrecht Cave.

Drive northwest 277mi (447km) to Willunga, where you'll start the Epicurean Way road trip that links great food and wine destinations in the Adelaide Hills, Barossa Valley, and Clare Valley. Along the way, stop off to enjoy some of South Australia's best food, wine, and beer.

Drive along the Limestone Coast for incredible coastal views, and stop at Canunda National Park for a bushwalk along the Coola Outstation Historical Walk, or Beachport Conservation Park to stay at 3 Mile Bend Campground and observe a variety of water birds on the lake.

Wet a line on the Murray River

The Murray River is Australia's longest, spanning an incredible 1,558mi (2,508km) across New South Wales, Victoria and South Australia. But, there's no better place to enjoy a spot of fishing and kayaking than

> " Follow the Eyre Peninsula Seafood Trail between Whyalla and Ceduna; along the way, try fresh prawns, oysters, lobsters, tuna, and more.

Port Lincoln

Getty Images/Kieran Stone

in South Australia. In the small city of Murray Bridge, an hours' drive from Adelaide, hire a kayak, pack a picnic, and paddle along the river to find the perfect picnic spot. You can fish here for Murray cod, callop, catfish, bream and redfin. Pack a fishing rod and try your luck at Katarapko Creek for golden perch and yabbies, or at Mungabareena for large river-dwelling trout.

Riverboat trips along the Murray leave from Adelaide daily, and range from three hours to a week.

Sea lion pups
Getty Images – by wildestanimal

Go diving with sharks and sea lions

South Australia has some phenomenal dive sites along its coast, but many people head to Port Lincoln to go cage diving with Great White sharks around the Neptune Islands. If that sounds too terrifying for you, try swimming with sea lions at Grindal Island or Hopkins, just offshore from Lincoln National Park.

Explore the Fleurieu Peninsula

There is great snorkeling, diving, fishing, and sailing on the Fleurieu Peninsula. Beginner and experienced divers will love the variety of dive sites, such as ex *HMAS Hobart* which was sunk in 2002 to make an artificial reef.

On the lower end of the Peninsula, Rapid Bay is a seaside community with a beautiful beach. Snorkelers may get a glimpse of a leafy sea dragon, a seahorse that is unique to the region. You can also take a sea

cave kayak tour to visit a local colony of inquisitive Long Nosed Fur-seals.

Naracoorte Caves National Park

South Australia's only World Heritage Site, Naracoorte Caves National Park is a vast cave system. Book a tour to learn about the resident bats and fossil-filled chambers.

If you're a caver, go straight to the Starburst Chamber and Fox Cave to crawl your way through with an experienced guide. You'll learn about the history and geology along the way. If you're new to the sport, book a novice tour to build your confidence. Always read your travel insurance policy wording to be sure if you're covered to do these activities.

Ikara-Flinders Ranges National Park

South Australia is no slouch when it comes to natural wonders. All it takes

Try swimming with sea lions at Grindal Island or Hopkins, just offshore from Lincoln National Park.

054

Wilpena Pound

Getty Images/tim phillips photos

is one trip into the Flinders Ranges to discover there's a whole world beyond the state's famous wine regions.

The start of the southern Outback, the Flinders Ranges is easy to get to from Adelaide via a quick flight or a five-hour drive. Stop in the Clare Valley along the way for fine food and wine. Once in the ranges, you'll find a wilderness with vast expanses of desert, massive cliffs, rocky hiking trails, deep gorges and a surprising number of birds, reptiles and mammals that survive in this rugged landscape.

Take to the skies on a Chinta Air Tour to see the extraordinary Wilpena Pound from above. This extraordinary natural rock amphitheater of mountains is hugely popular with rock climbers and bush walkers. On the ground, watch for emus, parrots, grey kangaroos and yellow-footed wallabies. Stay in an eco-villa at the Rawnsley Park Station and you're likely to have those friendly creatures right outside your door.

Take a hike in South Australia

Walk the short 1.4mi (2.4km) Ridge Trail in Mount George Conservation Park that leads to a rocky outcrop at the summit of Mount George for views over Bridgewater to Mount Lofty. Or take the very short 0.3mi (0.5km) walk to the summit of Mount Barker to see the countryside of Adelaide Hills, Porongurup Range, Stirling Ranges and the town of Mount Barker below.

If you're looking for a challenge, take a hike to the top of one of the highest peaks in South Flinders Ranges, Mount Brown (3,162ft/964m). The loop hike including the spur trail to Mount Brown is 9.3mi (15km), and should take approximately 7.5 hours to complete. Not only will you be treated to spectacular views of Flinders Ranges from the top, but you may even end up with a

“

The start of the southern Outback, the Flinders Ranges are easy to get from Adelaide via a quick flight or a five-hour drive.

Coober Pedy

> Guided by residents, you can tour some of the underground homes, or "dugouts" as the locals call them.

couple of mountain goats as hiking companions. The trail is flanked by large, majestic River Red Gum trees.

In the Dutchmans Stern Conservation Park, a five-hour return hike to the summit of Dutchmans Stern will really test your endurance. This 6.5mi (10.6km) moderate hike is worth it for views of the Spencer Gulf and the Willochra Plain from the top.

Coober Pedy

The small Outback town of Coober Pedy is the opal mining capital of the world but only has a few thousand residents. Due to the overwhelming heat during summer months (December to February), many people live in underground homes, dug out of the rock. No matter what the temperature was outside, these homes remain at a comfortable temperature.

Guided by residents, you can tour some of the underground homes, or "dugouts" as the locals call them. If you want to experience what it's like to live in an underground home, spend the night in one of the many underground accommodation options.

WOMADelaide and Adelaide Festival

Culture vultures should make a beeline for WOMADelaide, a four-day celebration of multicultural music and art. You can also engage in talks about the environment and sustainability or take part in workshops of soul capoeira or yoga.

The annual Adelaide Festival attracts an eclectic mix of outstanding performers, celebrates creative excellence, and draws huge arts-loving crowds. Both festivals run every March.

Stop by the Outback Pub, William Creek Hotel

Around 100 miles (160km) from the opal mining town of Coober Pedy, and halfway along the rugged Oodnadatta Track, South Australia's William Creek Hotel is not just a pub but also a one-stop-shop service center. A place to eat, drink, buy fuel, book a scenic flight, pick up souvenirs and more, this simple pub is a hub for travelers who find themselves in the remote outpost famously home to a population of six people and one dog. Under the rusty corrugated iron roof, you'll find cool ales, hot meals and a place to leave your mark by planting a sticker on the wall or hanging a hat from the ceiling.

Northern Territory

A rich Indigenous history and culture is waiting to be explored in the Northern Territory, a vast area with wildlife and natural wonders like nowhere else in the country.

Ormiston Gorge

Getty Images/Bryce Thomas

Food in the Northern Territory

From a pub meal in the Outback to Asian dishes in Darwin, a wide range of food is on offer around the Northern Territory. Mindil Beach Sunset Market in Darwin is a great place to sample food from around the world, such as crepes, kebabs, Indian dishes, and more. Daly Waters Pub first opened in 1930 and is one of the most famous stops along the Stuart Highway. While you're there, try the Barramundi sandwich.

Check the menu carefully if you're looking for something uniquely Australian, as many restaurants around the state also serve meat from crocodiles, camels, emus, and kangaroos. Kangaroo is very rich and lean, best cooked medium-rare, while crocodile meat is very pale and tastes like chicken. Camel and emu meat taste similar to beef and is best eaten on a burger.

Culture in the Northern Territory

Alice Springs is the cultural hub of the Red Center. Just outside of town, you'll find the Alice Springs Telegraph Station that was established in 1871 to relay telegraph messages from Darwin to Adelaide. Downtown, you'll find incredible Aboriginal art in many of the art galleries in Todd Mall and the Araluen Galleries. Before buying any art, ensure the dealer follows the Indigenous art code or buy directly from the artist at a community art center.

Located 62mi (100km) offshore from Darwin, the Tiwi Islands are home to the Tiwi people, one of

Road Trip Ideas

Driving the Northern Territory from Alice Springs to Darwin via the Stuart Highway is one of the classic Northern Territory road trips, and will take you from the red dirt of the desert to the coral reefs in the Arafura Sea. There are plenty of places to stop along the 932mi (1,500km) route to break up the drive, including Karlu Karlu (Devils Marbles), Daly Waters Pub, and Katherine Gorge.

Take the long way to Uluru from Alice Springs and visit Kings Canyon, Kata Tjuta, and Finke Gorge National Park, where the Finke River, one of the oldest waterways in the world, flows. Peer into Tnorala (Gosse Bluff), a comet crater that's more than 140 million years old.

Driving the Savannah Way, from Cairns to Broome, is one of Australia's most epic road trip routes. Drive the 2,175mi (3,501km), to see the best the Australian Outback has to offer. If you're driving a 4WD, you can explore remote parts of the Outback, see the sandstone spires in Cape Crawford before visiting Borroloola, one of Australia's most remote towns, which is also home to excellent fishing. On the other side of Katherine, Flora River Nature Park is one of the best barramundi fishing destinations in the NT. Catch your dinner and roast it over a campfire under the stars.

Australia's Indigenous groups. Tours leave from Darwin, by plane or ferry, and include morning tea with the Tiwi women, a stop at a Tiwi burial site, and a traditional smoking ceremony, performed by the women of the community to bless their visitors.

Mary River

An hour's drive from Darwin, Mary River Wilderness Retreat is a great spot for bushwalking, with trails for all fitness levels from the 1mi (1.6km) Wallaby Walk to the 4mi (6.4km) River Walk. If you have time, drive a further 45 minutes to Mary River National Park for more bushwalking trails and vast wildlife-rich billabongs, including Mistake Billabong. However, it's not for swimming; Mary River is infested with crocodiles.

Kakadu National Park

Covering more than 7,722mi^2 (20,000km^2) the World Heritage site of Kakadu National Park is considered one of the best national parks in the world. With incredible biodiversity, Kakadu is filled with wildlife and dramatic rugged landscapes. Search for crocodiles and birds in Corroboree Billabong, watch the sunset in Ubirr, and take a dip in nature's infinity pool at Gunlom Falls.

The Bininj and Mungguy people have lived in Kakadu for more than 50,000 years, and the local rock art is some of the best in the country. Nourlangie is home to the famous Lightning Man Creation Ancestor

Litchfield National Park

Kate McIntosh

where you'll see lots of hand art, figures hunting, and more. Look for the Tasmanian tiger at Ubirr, where the smooth stone surfaces were perfect for painting.

Litchfield National Park

A 90-minute drive from Darwin, Litchfield National Park is much smaller than Kakadu, and makes for a great day trip. Cool off by taking a wild swim at Florence Falls, the Buley Rockhole or Wangi Falls. Most swimming sites in the Northern Territory are only accessible during the dry season. During the wet season, crocodiles find their way into many of the waterways. Never go swimming if there's a warning sign, and always check to be sure these places aren't sacred to local Indigenous tribes.

On a typical humid day in the park, splash in the rock pools of Buley Rockhole before walking the 1.9mi (3.2km) Florence Creek Walking trail to Florence Falls, where (again) you can take a swim under the waterfall.

> " Search for crocodiles and birds in Corroboree Billabong, watch the sunset in Ubirr, and take a dip in nature's infinity pool at Gunlom Falls.

Uluru

Robin Falls

Take a drive to this quiet waterfall, a 90-minute drive from Darwin. This is a rare gem where you won't find any tour groups, but don't be surprised if you spot the odd (harmless) water snake or water monitor. It's a great place to cool off after going on a must-do Jumping Crocodile Cruise on the Adelaide River.

Sweets Lagoon

Sweets Lagoon is famous for its iconic five-meter-long, territorial crocodile, Sweetheart, who used to chew motors off boats in the 1970s. You can visit his former home to see the vast floodplain and spot wildlife with Outback Floatplane Adventures, which can fly you to the remote area and tour you by airboat. Though, at US $500, the tours aren't cheap. Alternatively, stop in at the Windows on the Wetlands, a lookout point with interactive exhibits. It also offers free nature walks on weekends during the dry season.

Uluru

In the heart of the Red Center (and Australia), Uluru is one of the great natural wonders of the world, rising 1,141ft (348m) out of the desert. Uluru is an important spiritual place for the local Anangu people, who are the traditional owners of Uluru. Visitors are asked not to climb the rock as the path follows the same walked by initiated senior Indigenous men, the Mala. An official climbing ban comes into effect in October 2019 out of respect to local custom. The climb is also incredibly dangerous and has resulted in the deaths of more than 30 people. For a much better appreciation of the famous

> " Visitors are asked not to climb the rock as the path follows the same walked by initiated senior Indigenous men, the Mala.

Grab a Feed at the Daly Waters Pub

Bring your sense of humor to this one-of-a-kind watering hole found 560 miles (901km) north of Alice Springs. Sitting just off the Stuart Highway, this pub shows zero restraint when it comes to interior decoration. Bras hang from the ceiling, flip-flops are strung up in the beer garden and stickers cover every square inch of the bar. Find a spot at the bar, order a cold beer and ask the publican about the pub's chequered past – since the 1930s, the pub has seen brawls, murders, robberies and cattle stampedes.

Katherine Gorge
Getty Images/Whitworth Images

The Rim Walk starts with a difficult climb uphill before you reach the top of the canyon. Halfway along, stop to see (swimming isn't allowed) the waterhole surrounded by rare plants in the "Garden of Eden", and walk in the shade of ancient palms that dot the length of the trail.

Nitmiluk National Park

Home to Katherine Gorge, Nitmiluk National Park belongs to the Jawoyn and Dagomen people. In its 13 gorges, there are Indigenous rock paintings on the sandstone walls featuring x-ray-style art. Hire a canoe to see them on the canyon walls, or cool off with a dip at Leliyn (Edith Falls).

The Jatbula Trail is a 36mi (58km) multi-day trek that starts at the visitor center and ends at Leliyn. The trail passes ancient Aboriginal rock art, waterfalls, monsoon rainforest, and takes about four days to complete. The trek can be completed with or without a guide, and you should expect to carry all your equipment and food, walking approximately 6–10mi (10–17km) a day.

Walk the Larapinta Trail

The Larapinta Trail is 138.5mi (223km) long, and winds through the West MacDonnell Ranges. The trek typically takes 12 days to complete. Due to the intense heat, the best time of year to attempt it is between May and August. Many people choose to walk smaller sections as a day hike. The trail is challenging and remote, so carry equipment, water, and food.

monolith, take the 6.2mi (10km) Uluru Base Walk, or wake up early a catch a colorful sunrise from Dune Walk Lookout.

Kata Tjuta

A 45-minute drive from Uluru, Kata Tjuta is a 36-dome rock formation that is as beautiful as Uluru but has fewer crowds. The Valley of the Winds walk winds through the heart of Kata Tjuta offers incredible views of the ancient landscape. There are many Dreamtime legends associated with Kata Tjuta, but the most shared story is about the great snake king, Wanambi, who is said to live on the summit of Kata Tjuta. Many of the traditional stories of the Anangu are not usually shared with outsiders as is the custom.

Watarrka National Park

Take a three-hour drive north of Uluru to Kings Canyon in Watarrka National Park. Lace up your hiking boots and discover the natural beauty of the 328ft (100m) sandstone walls of the canyon on the 3.7mi (6km) Rim Walk.

The Jatbula Trail is a 36mi (58km) multi-day trek that starts at the visitor center and ends at Leliyn. The trail passes ancient Aboriginal rock art, waterfalls, monsoon rainforest, and takes about four days to complete.

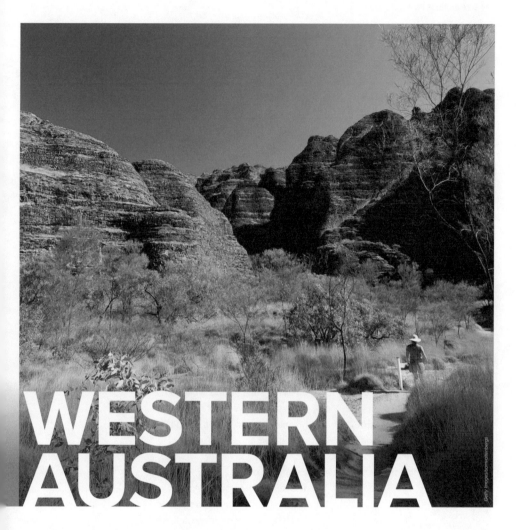

Getty Images/stonenollenbergs

WESTERN AUSTRALIA

The guide books will all tell you to see Wave Rock, The Pinnacles, Margaret River and, of course, the city of Perth. But in a state this diverse, there are so many other incredible destinations to explore. Head away from the city and the visitor hotspots to discover Australia's biggest state.

Western Australia

An incredible coastline, a pristine reef and extraordinary opportunities to observe wildlife, plus national parks and stunning natural wonders make this huge state an adventurer's paradise.

Exmouth and the Ningaloo reef

Getty Images/SommyVision

Elephant Rocks

On the far south coast of the state, William Bay National Park lies around 10mi (16km) west of the town of Denmark. The park has a number of beaches, coves and rock formations which many travelers bypass on the road to Albany. Perhaps most famous are Elephant Rocks, a group of large rocks resembling a herd of elephants wading out to sea. The rocks are only a short walk from a car park, but nearby Greens Pool, where round boulders naturally shelter the bay from crashing waves, makes a great place to swim in the calm water.

Waterfall Beach has a unique freshwater waterfall cascading directly onto the sand, and Madfish Bay is another great place to go swimming and fishing. Both can be accessed by 2WD, but note that reaching them requires driving on corrugated and sandy tracks.

Esperance

The town of Esperance acts as a hub to refuel, refresh and restock before heading into one of many national parks that litter the southern coast of Western Australia. Take a day trip from Esperance to follow Twilight Beach Road and explore the coves along the coastline.

Further east, head 29mi (46km) to Cape Le Grand National Park to share the sand with kangaroos at Lucky Bay, picnic among the sand dunes and heathlands of Hellfire Bay

> " Take a day trip from Esperance to follow Twilight Beach Road and explore the coves along the coastline.

Getty Images/John Crux Photography

Twilight Beach near Esperance

Getty Images/John Crux Photography

The Pinnacles, Nambung National Park

and Thistle Cove, or, 4WD on the beach at Cape Le Grand.

Inland, Frenchman Peak is a well-paced, 1.8mi (3km) hike that rewards with sweeping views back across the park. Along with kangaroos, emus can be found roaming the pristine sands of Lucky Bay, and offshore, whales can be seen basking in the shallows. Lucky Bay was also selected as having the whitest sand in Australia in 2017.

See incredible pink lakes

There are a number of pink lakes across Australia, some natural and some artificial (which are used as Beta-Carotene farms). Created by a combination of high salt levels, algae, and brine shrimp, pink lakes can be found at the Hutt Lagoon on the road to Kalbarri and also just below the Collier Ranges, although they are often dry. The Pink Lake, 2mi (3km)

How Exmouth Became the World's Cleanest Beach

Conservation has always been key for the people of Exmouth, in Western Australia. Here, the locals show great pride in the natural beauty of their town and coast, the jumping-off point for pristine Ningaloo Reef. More than a decade ago plastic bags were banned, and local schools launched initiatives to teach the next generation about sustainable waste management.

Exmouth's government officials, activists and locals are already way ahead in their dedication to making not only the city's Town Beach a pristine place, but to keeping other beaches in the North West Cape and the UNESCO World Heritage-listed area of the Ningaloo Coast, free of trash, pollutants and plastics.

Massive Community Involvement Is the Key

Since the initial plastic-bag ban 10 years ago, local people have been responsible for making the beauty of the area's beaches legendary around the world. It was, explains Exmouth Shire President Matthew Niikkula, "a voluntary community initiative, supported by local residents and embraced by visitors to the area. The Exmouth community is very aware of the importance of our natural environment and the need to protect its unique World Heritage values."

So not only do the people of Exmouth take their own bags when they shop, they go much further. "Since February 2016, I have been organizing beach cleans as part of Sea Shepherd's Marine Debris Campaign," explains Grace Keast, the Sea Shepherd Chapter Coordinator for Exmouth. "There are many different beaches along the coast of this peninsula, so we go to a different one each month. We choose the beach by the level of footfall or from reports from people witnessing rubbish accumulating. To this end, we have conducted 12 cleans with 131 volunteers."

west of Esperance, may have lost much of its once bubblegum pink color, but it could be slowly returning, and the lake is worth checking out while driving the scenic Twilight Beach Road.

Lake Hillier is a far more vibrant pink lake located on Middle Island, part of Cape Arid National Park. Due to its remoteness, the best way to see the lake is via a scenic tour from Esperance.

Coral Bay, Exmouth & Ningaloo Reef

Coral Bay is a small settlement on the northwest coast. Previously known as Maud's Bay, after the first European ship to visit the area, the town took its current name from a local hotel in the 1960s. There are numerous sites to snorkel off the beach, but, for those more confident, head just offshore to the spot known as Ayers Rock for better visibility and often, greater numbers of reef fish.

There are also numerous tour companies in Coral Bay, ranging from eco-friendly reef and wildlife tours, to dune buggies and quad biking. The UNESCO World Heritage Ningaloo Reef runs close to the coast, and there are opportunities to swim alongside whale sharks, whales and manta rays.

The dunes south of the town are a popular spot for four-wheel driving, complete with basic campsites scattered along the beaches and coves.

The Ningaloo Reef lies just off

Whale Shark, Ningaloo Reef
Ningaloo Discovery

Coral Bay, making the town a popular place for scuba diving charters, snorkeling, eco tours and sailing. Stretching more than 160mi (257km) along the far northwest coast, as a fringing reef, you can walk off the beach in many places to snorkel. The Ningaloo Reef is also famous for boat tours that take visitors out just beyond the reef, between March and June, to swim alongside extraordinary, huge whale sharks. Other marine life including dugongs, dolphins, humpback whales and manta rays can also be seen.

Shark Bay

The World Heritage site of Shark Bay is an exceptional place to see dugongs and dolphins, and the natural phenomena, stromatolites, littering Hamelin Pool. Shark Bay is also home to Monkey Mia, where travelers can learn about the significance of the area to local

> 66
> The Ningaloo Reef is also famous for boat tours that take visitors out just beyond the reef, between March and June, to swim alongside extraordinary, huge whale sharks.

Indigenous people as part of an eco-tour. Visit Eagle Bluff Lookout, where you may be lucky enough to spot sharks, rays and turtles in the clear water below. For those seeking the opportunity to hand-feed wild dolphins, the closely monitored marine park offers just that.

Kalbarri National Park

Around 96mi (154km) north of Geraldton, Kalbarri National Park is home to the Murchison River, river gorges, dramatic coastal cliffs and beaches, coastal and inland hiking trails and off-road activities including quad biking and four-wheel driving. There are no campsites in the park, but there is accommodation in the coastal town of Kalbarri.

Check out the Z Bend River Trail, which ends at a great gorge lookout, and The Loop Track, where you can see the Natures Window rock formation. While hiking, keep an eye out for echidnas, kangaroos and emus. Along the river, you might see bearded dragons, hopping mice, and

Natures Window rock formation in Kalbarri National Park

dragonflies, and you can hire a kayak to see nature while paddling through the water.

Along the coast, stop by Mushroom Rock, Eagle Gorge, and Red Bluff before relaxing on the beach at sunset. If you're searching for a beach campsite, you can rest for the night at Lucky Bay, which is on the road to Kalbarri.

Karijini National Park

Take a long drive 650mi (1,046km) north of Perth to the World Heritage site of Karijini National Park, where you can explore vast wilderness areas that include gorges, rock formations, hiking trails and swimming holes.

At Dales Gorge, take a hike to see Fortescue Falls and Fern Pool, both sites that hold significance for the local Indigenous people. There's a

Knox Gorge, Karijini National Park

> Take a long drive 650mi (1,046km) north of Perth to the World Heritage site of Karijini National Park

campground close to Dales Gorge, in case you arrive late in the day and want to stay overnight.

Don't miss Hancock Gorge, further east, and Knox Gorge, accessed via an unsealed road. Both offer great lookouts and trails where you'll see the unique rock layers in the park. Descend into Hancock Gorge, via a steep ladder, to swim in beautiful Kermit's Pool.

In the southern part of the park, walk to the summit of Mount Bruce in time to catch the sunrise. A steady two-hour hike will seem like nothing once you reach the top and see the vibrant colors of the Outback at dawn. Check the trails are open before you set off.

Champagne Springs, El Questro

Getty Images/samvoltenbergs

Broome

Broome sits on the northwest coast of Western Australia, close to the natural wonders of the Kimberley region. Famous for stunning sunsets at Cable Beach, Broome is a great place to base yourself before heading east into the Kimberley or to Purnululu National Park.

Broome once had a thriving pearling industry, and each year, the Shinju Matsuri Festival is held in late August and September to celebrate the fusion of European, Japanese, Chinese and South Asian cultures that arrived here during the city's pearling heyday. Roebuck Bay is home to large colonies of seabirds, and, at low tide, fossilized dinosaur footprints can be seen along areas of the coastline and the mudflats off Gantheaume Point.

Between March and November, a unique phenomenon called the 'Staircase to the Moon' can be seen from Broome. The moon rising over exposed mudflats forms a truly breathtaking sight. Check for the best dates and times to see it while you're visiting.

Horizontal Falls

In Talbot Bay, in the far north of the Kimberley region, the world-famous Horizontal Falls are formed by rising tides and water levels on either side of narrow passes, leading into an enclosed lagoon. As the water rises quickly on one side of the pass, powerful whirlpools are formed, creating the horizontal waterfalls. One of the most intriguing natural wonders to be seen in Australia, the falls can be viewed via boat and

" Between March and November, a unique phenomenon called the 'Staircase to the Moon' can be seen from Broome. The moon rising over exposed mudflats forms a truly breathtaking sight.

plane tours operating from Derby, but are best viewed from the water.

El Questro

The Kimberley region in Western Australia's far north is pure wilderness, untamed and remote. About 64mi (102km) west of Kununurra, visit El Questro Wilderness Park to experience what has been described as Australia's last frontier. The landscapes are incredible, with dramatic mountains, winding gorges, thermal springs, swimming holes, rainforest and waterfalls. Hire a 4WD and stock up on supplies before heading out to one of the campsites including Kingfisher Camp, the luxurious El Questro homestead or El Questro Station.

There are dozens of hiking trails within a short distance of each campsite, but don't miss Amalia Gorge, El Questro Gorge or the swimming holes at Jackaroo's Hole and Moonshine Gorge. You can camp, stay in a simple bungalow or go all out and enjoy the Homestead, in your own villa perched on the edge of Chamberlain Gorge. You can cruise along the gorge, climb to Zebedee Thermal Springs for a cooling dip in a tree-lined hideaway, or go on a fascinating guided bushwalk that culminates in a sunset toast high above El Questro's 700,000 of untamed wilderness.

Remember, some 4WD trails may require creek crossings, which shouldn't be attempted without the

Campervan on the beach near Broome
Getty Images/Westend61

right equipment for your vehicle.

Cathedral Gorge, Purnululu National Park

In the heart of the Bungle Bungles, hike across the surreal countryside with a local Indigenous guide to hear the cultural stories of the region. Walk into Cathedral Gorge, a massive red-rock amphitheater, with amazing acoustics, that will make you feel very small – but your voice will echo to the sky beyond.

> In northern Western Australia, hundreds of campsites dot the shoreline and national parks, some basic and others with excellent facilities.

Go Camping in Western Australia

In northern Western Australia, hundreds of campsites dot the shoreline and national parks, some basic and others with excellent facilities. If you're looking for somewhere wild and remote, try Gregories at the tip of Cape Peron, or Kurrajong, Osprey or Yardie Homestead in Cape Range National Park.

Explore the sand roads in a self-contained camper north of Broome or in the King Leopold Ranges. Stay the night at Charnley River Station or Silent Grove.

In southwest Australia, go camping at Lucky Bay and Cape Le Grand Beach. Further east, set up camp at Yokinup campground, located in Cape Arid National Park.

Most campsites that offer facilities require a fee, but many wilderness camps can be used free of charge – just double check online ahead of time.

Download the Wikicamps app to use offline, so you can find major and minor campsites throughout Australia. If you're on a last-minute hunt for a site nearby, it could be a lifesaver.

Essential Insurance Tips

Ignoring the practicalities of traveling through a large, remote and often very hot and dry country has caught out many experienced travelers. Here are a few things to know about your insurance cover before you travel around Australia.

Protect your gear from theft

Australians are renowned for their welcoming attitude and it's with good reason, however, while the majority are friendly to travelers, some are more interested in your wallet than getting to know you.

Theft is a common claim in Australia. It takes just seconds for a thief to grab your camera or wallet from under your beach towel at Bondi while you're swimming, or off the table while you're ordering coffee. Always keep your valuables on you or locked up (using the hotel safe or hostel lockers). Also don't leave anything in your car as break and enters are common in urban areas (especially at night). If your belongings aren't with you, and there is no evidence or police report of a theft, you may not be covered if they're stolen.

Travel insurance isn't designed to cover everything, particularly if you leave something behind or, on some insurance plans, if your gear is damaged. Check your policy carefully for full details of cover, including the limit payable on each item, the excess (your contribution or deductible) and any exclusions or conditions of cover such as depreciation or valid proof of ownership.

Baggage delay

Australia's remoteness is part of its charm but can also present some challenges if your baggage is delayed. Most visitors require a half-day plane ride to get to Australia, so you're unlikely to get your baggage back quickly if your airline has delivered it to Sidney, Canada instead of Sydney, Australia.

Most travel insurance policies can help replace essentials, like a change of clothes or toothbrush, if you have to wait more than 24 hours for your bags to arrive. Travel insurance isn't designed to swap your ripped jeans for a designer pair, so read this section of your policy carefully before you spend up big and then try and claim.

Before you leave home, ensure your baggage is clearly labelled and the tags are firmly attached, giving your airline the best chance of getting it on the right plane or finding it quickly and getting it back to you.

> Theft is a common claim in Australia. It takes just seconds for a thief to grab your camera or wallet from under your beach towel at Bondi while you're swimming, or off the table while you're ordering coffee.

Real-claim story

"I was in the stall of a washroom with my bag in front of me, within arm's reach. While I was using the toilet, my bag containing my electronics was pulled from under the door by an unknown person. By the time I pulled up my pants and went outside, no one was there. I went to the Police immediately and filed a report."

Canadian resident in Australia.

Medical insurance for accidents or injuries

The Australian medical system is first class, but it comes with a price, so make sure you take out a full medical travel insurance plan before you travel.

This is different to the medical insurance cover you might have at home which won't cover you overseas. Medical Insurance is your safety net if you become very unwell; it's not designed to pay for every scratch and headache, which is why benefit limits and excesses apply.

If you're hurt or injured, contact us for assistance and we can help you understand what your policy covers. You may decide, if your ailment is minor and under the excess, to not make a claim. If it's a life-threatening medical condition, always seek medical help immediately. Let us know as soon as you can what has happened so we can help you access medical assistance and keep your family and friends informed.

Adventure sport coverage

There are many great opportunities to do adventure sports in Australia, which is why our travel insurance covers hundreds of them from kite surfing to skiing and parasailing.

Policy exclusions do vary, so, depending on the level of cover you've purchased, read it carefully and make sure you're covered before you go bungee jumping in Cairns or scuba diving in Byron Bay.

If you get hurt skiing in the Victorian Alps, and it's not in your policy, it's going to be a very expensive trip.

Check your policy carefully so there are no surprises

Your travel insurance policy will have limits and exclusions. This ensures the policy you pay for is kept at a lower cost.

And, remember, if you do something really stupid, like grab a snake by the head or go swimming with crocodiles, you may not be covered at all.

Real-claim story

"My surfboard, which was packed in a proper travel board cover, was creased and snapped after being transported on plane."

Australian returning from overseas.

Made in United States
Troutdale, OR
02/15/2024